Buckle for Dust in association with
English Touring Theatre present

Hundreds and Thousands
by Lou Ramsden

UK premiere at Soho Theatre Upstairs, London, on 21 June 2011

Hundreds and Thousands

by Lou Ramsden

Cast

ALLAN	Stuart Laing
TIGGY	Nadine Lewington
LORNA	Sukie Smith
JONATHAN	Robert Wilfort

Creative Team

Director	Lisa Spirling
Designer	Polly Sullivan
Lighting Designer	Tim Mascall
Sound Designer	Gregory Clarke
Assistant Director	Tinuke Craig
Stage Manager	Lorna Seymour
Assistant Stage Manager	Amy Wildgoose
Production Manager	Andy Stubbs
Casting	Annelie Powell
Producers	Claire Birch and Ali Taylor
Production Assistant	Babs Iles
Carpenters	Bob Belson and Nick Stewart
Graphic Designers	Radford Wallis
Photography	Graham Michael

The Company

Stuart Laing (*Allan*)

Theatre includes: *The Furies / Land of the Dead* (Dialogue Productions); *Blowing Whistles* (Leicester Square Theatre); *Drowning on Dry Land* (Salisbury Playhouse); *Season's Greetings* (Liverpool Playhouse); *A Streetcar Named Desire* (Theatr Clwyd); *Indian Summer* (Sgript Cymru); *Billy and the Crab Lady*, *Food for Thought* (Soho); *Hushabye Mountain* (ETC tour); *Trouble with Girls* (NT Studio); *Kiss of the Spiderwoman* (Leicester Haymarket); *Over Here* (Leicester Haymarket Studio/tour); *Loot* (Thorndike Leatherhead); *Salt Lake Psycho* (Man in the Moon); *Bad Company* (Bush).

Television includes: *How TV Ruined your Life* (Zeppotron Ltd); *Doctors*, *EastEnders*, *Inspector Lynley*, *Holby City*, *Spooks*, *Everytime You Look at Me*, *Cambridge Spies*, *Stag*, *In the Land of Plenty*, *Berkeley Square*, *Love Bites – In Your Dreams*, *Devil's Advocate*, *Casualty* (BBC); *The Bill* (Thames); *Trial and Retribution* (La Plante Productions); *The Animator* (IWC Media); *Vincent*, *Wire in the Blood*, *Frances Tuesday*, *Poirot: Sad Cypress*, *Bob Martin* (Granada); *Sex and Lies* (Blast! Films); *Murphy's Law* (Tiger Aspect); *Burn It* (Red Productions); *In Between* (Indica Films Ltd); *The Listener* (MK Productions); *Heartbeat*, *Strike Force*, *Blood and Peaches* (YTV); *Kavanagh QC* (Carlton); *Minder* (Euston Films).

Film includes: *Lie Still* (Indobrit Pictures Ltd); *The Great Ecstasy of Robert Carmichael* (Pullback Camera); *Nine Songs* (Revolution Films); *Butterfly Man* (De Warrenne Pictures); *The Lawless Heart* (MP Productions); *SW9* (Fruit Salad Films); *Truth Game*, *Strong Language* (Rumley Films); *Gaston's War* (Era Films); *Three Steps to Heaven* (Maya Vision).

Nadine Lewington (*Tiggy*)

Nadine is best known for her role as Dr Maddy Young in BBC1's *Holby City*. Other television and film includes: *Doctors*, *Family Affairs*, *Casualty*, *Dream Team*, *What If*, *All in Good Time*, and *Contraction*.

Audio includes: *Doctor Who* and *Rubbish Men*.

Presenting includes: Kiss FM 105-108.

Nadine most recently played Asta Allmers in *Little Eyolf* at the Jermyn Street Theatre.

Sukie Smith (*Lorna*)

Theatre includes: *Garage Band* (Nottingham Playhouse); *My Mother Said I Never Should* (West Yorkshire Playhouse); *A Girl in a Car With a Man* (Royal Court); *Keepers* (Hampstead); *Rhinoceros, Here is the Monster* (Man in the Moon); *Claptrap, On the Side of Angels* (Edinburgh); *The Country Wife* (Holland Park Theatre); *La Bête* (Lyric, Hammersmith); *Temptation* (West End).

Television includes: *The Yellow House, Innocents* (Channel 4); *EastEnders, My Hero, The Queen's Nose, Casualty* (BBC); *The New Adventures of Robin Hood* (US TV); *The Paul Merton Show, Peak Practice* (Carlton); *The Bill* (Thames); *Inspector Morse* (Central).

Film includes: *The Rides, The Lawless Heart, Topsy Turvy, Peggy Su!, Wedlock, Enchanted April, Asking for It, The Witches and a Summer Story, Green Hut, Gyppo, This One's for Me, Shadow Buddy, Straight, The Early Days, 875, Hoppy.*

Radio includes: *All God's Children, Her Father's Daughter, Say It With Flowers* (BBC).

Robert Wilfort (*Jonathan*)

Theatre includes: *Present Laughter* (Theatr Clwyd); *The Jollies* (Stephen Joseph); *Sense and Sensibility* (Exeter Northcott); *School of Night, Semi-Detached* (Chichester Festival).

Television includes: *Campus, Skins, Clitheroe* (Channel 4); *Ashes to Ashes, DOA* (Pilot); *Gavin and Stacey, The Persuasionists, Casualty, Beautiful People, Raging, Pulling, Broken News, Cake: Brief Encounters, Holby City, Grass, High Hopes* (BBC); *Coronation Street, Friends and Crocodiles, Murder Most Horrid* (ITV); *Heartbeat* (YTV); *The Bill* (Thames); *The Commander* (La Plant Productions); *Large* (Presentable Production); *Lucky Jim* (Working Title Films); *Blonde Bombshell* (LWT).

Film includes: *Eight Minutes Idle* (Cinema Six); *Me and Orson Welles* (Cinema NX); *Harry Potter and the Goblet of Fire* (Warner Brothers); *The Libertine* (Libertine Films Ltd); *All or Nothing* (Thin Man Films); *Happy Now* (Ruby Films).

Lou Ramsden (Writer)

Lou is an artistic director of Buckle for Dust. She is currently one of the '503 Five', a group of writers on attachment with Theatre503. Her first full-length play *Breed* was produced there in September 2010 and she was subsequently shortlisted for the Critics' Circle Most Promising Playwright Award.

Other theatre includes: *2004* (part of *DECADE* at Theatre503); *Gas and Air* (Edinburgh Festival Fringe and Pleasance Theatre, London); *Black Snot* (Royal Court Young Writers' Festival, Jerwood Theatre Upstairs); *The Devil of Great Titchfield Street* (Paines Plough Wild Lunch, Young Vic).

Radio includes: *Dos and Don'ts for the Mentally Interesting* (MIND Mental Health Media Award 2009); *Blood in the Bridal Shop, In Form, Gunpowder Women, Lilly's Mum, Tree Splitting, Sampler T6* and *Pouring Poison*.

Lisa Spirling (Director)

Lisa is an artistic director of Buckle For Dust and an affiliate artist of Theatre503. She is the recipient of a Creative Industries Award from The Hospital Club. She trained at LAMDA, Royal Holloway University of London and NT Studio.

Directing credits include: *Coalition* (Theatre503); *Boeing Boeing* (Alley Theatre, Houston); *Terminal Four Play* (Theatre503, Latitude Festival); *Cotton Wool* (Buckle for Dust at Theatre503, Meyer-Whitworth Award winner); *Idiots of Ants* (Pleasance, Edinburgh, and on tour; Eddy nominated 2009); *Beowulf* (Storm on the Lawn, Theatre Royal Bath); *Beauty and the Beast* (Jacksons Lane); *The Vagina Monologues* (Pleasance, London); *No One Move* (Barons Court); *Gas and Air* and *New York Threesome* (Edinburgh Fringe and Pleasance, London).

Associate directing credits include: *In a Forest Dark and Deep* (Nimax, West End); *ENRON* (Director of 2nd cast; Headlong and ACT, West End and national tour); *The Hypochondriac* (Liverpool Playhouse and English Touring Theatre).

Assistant directing credits include: *Danton's Death* (National Theatre); *King Lear* (Headlong, Young Vic and Liverpool Everyman); *Boeing Boeing* (ACT, national tour).

Polly Sullivan (Designer)

Theatre includes: *Tactical Questioning, Called to Account* (Tricycle); *The Snow Dragon* (Tall Stories); *A Christmas Carol* (Chicken Shed); *Seduced* (Finborough); *The Atheist, Cotton Wool* (Theatre503); *The Lady of Burma* (Riverside Studios); *You Might As Well Live* (New End).

Tim Mascall (Lighting Designer)

Lighting design includes: *Ruby Wax: Losing It, Breakfast with Jonny Wilkinson*, (Menier Chocolate Factory); *A Doll's House* (Exeter Northcott); *The Importance of Being Earnest* (Regent's Park Open Air Theatre); *A Small Family Business* (Watford Palace); *How to Disappear Completely and Never Be Found* (Southwark Playhouse); *Marilyn and Ella* (Theatre Royal Stratford East); *Cotton Wool* (Theatre503); *Bells Are Ringing* (Union); *Vote Dizzy* (Soho); *Nora* (Mercury); *Lies Have Been Told: An Evening with Robert Maxwell* (Trafalgar Studios); *Jenufa* (Natural Perspective/Arcola); *Professor Bernhardi and Rose Bernd* (Oxford Stage Company); *The Importance of Being Earnest* (New Wolsey); and national tours of *Trainspotting, Pete and Dud: Come Again, Latin Fever, Stones in His Pockets, Off the Wall, Gizmo Love, Bad Jazz* (ATC).

West End designs include: *The Vagina Monologues* (Wyndhams); *Latin Fever* (Peacock); *Well* (Apollo); *Why the Whales Came* (Comedy).

Between 2007 and 2010 Tim designed the lighting for all of Derren Brown's live shows including *Enigma* (Adelphi); *Something Wicked This Way Comes* (Old Vic) and *An Evening of Wonder* (Garrick)

Gregory Clarke (Sound Designer)

Gregory won a Tony Award for Best Sound Design in a Play for *Equus* and received the New York Drama Desk Award for Outstanding Sound Design for *Journey's End*.

For the Royal Shakespeare Company: *The Merchant Of Venice, Cymbeline, Great Expectations, Coriolanus, The Merry Wives of Windsor, Tantalus*.

Other theatre includes: *Twelfth Night, Earthquakes in London* (National Theatre); *A Flea in Her Ear, Six Degrees of Separation* (Old Vic); *Penelope* (Druid tour); *Bedroom Farce, Rain Man* (West End); *Goodnight Mister Tom, A Month in the Country, Caught My Death in Venice, Nathan the Wise, Song of Singapore* (Chichester); *Peter Pan* (Kensington Gardens/O2 Centre/US tour); *A Midsummer Night's Dream, Treasure Island, Bedroom Farce, Miss Julie, The Browning Version, Love's Labour's Lost* (Rose); *The Philanthropist* (American Airlines, Broadway); *My Dad's a Birdman, Bay* (Young Vic); *For King and Country* (UK tour); *The Electric Ballroom* (Riverside Studios); *Loot* (Tricycle); *Crown Matrimonial, Ring around the Moon* (Act Productions); *Equus* (Gielgud/Broadway); *Jeffrey Bernard is Unwell, Blithe Spirit, The Rivals, Hedda Gabler, The Winslow Boy, Balmoral, The Browning Version, Swansong, The Apple Cart, Home, How the Other Half Loves, Victory, Old Times, Amy's View, You Never Can Tell, HMS Pinafore, Much Ado About Nothing, The Dresser, As You Like It* (Bath); *Where There's a Will, Uncle Vanya* (ETT); *Little Wolf, In the Club, The Glass Room, Everything is Illuminated, Clever Dick, When the Night Begins, Revelations, The Maths Tutor* (Hampstead); *Peter Pan, Krindlekrax,* (Birmingham Rep); *Cloud 9* (Almeida); *The Boyfriend, Lady Be Good, A Midsummer Night's Dream, Macbeth, Twelfth Night, Cymbeline* (NSC); *A Voyage Round my Father* (Donmar); *Hay Fever* (Haymarket); *Nights at the Circus* (Lyric Hammersmith); *National Anthems* (Old Vic).

Claire Birch (Creative Producer)

Claire is the creative producer at Buckle for Dust. She is also a freelance producer and the Associate Producer at ETT.

For ETT, productions include: *Eden End* (Royal and Derngate and national tour); *Little Baby Jesus* (Oval House/Latitude Festival); *Rum and Coca Cola* (West Yorkshire Playhouse/national tour); *Lovesong* (Brighton, Latitude and Edinburgh festivals/national tour); and various readings. She assisted on *The Grapes of Wrath* and *The Hypochondriac* (national tours).

Other producing credits include: *Mad Forest* (BAC, JMK Director Award show); *A Christmas Carol* (Jacksons Lane); *Dov and Ali, Cotton Wool* (Theatre503).

Claire produced the Royal Court Young Writers' Festival 2006/07, including two productions: *The Eleventh Capital* and the Olivier Award-winning *Gone Too Far*, as well as eight readings.

Lorna Seymour (Stage Manager)

Lorna studied English and Philosophy at Durham University, and Stage Management at RADA. She has worked as a freelance stage manager on a variety of theatre and opera productions, including the opening season at Soho Theatre in 2000, and six seasons at English National Opera.

Theatre includes: *Clybourne Park* (Royal Court/West End); *The Master Builder, Rope, When the Rain Stops Falling* (Almeida); *ENRON* (Chichester/Royal Court/West End); *King Lear* (Liverpool Everyman/Young Vic); *Macbeth* (Chichester/West End/New York).

Tinuke Craig (Assistant Director)

Tinuke Craig is a freelance theatre director. She began directing at the University of Sussex and went on to train as a director at the London Academy of Music and Dramatic Art (LAMDA), graduating in 2010. Tinuke is a script reader for Theatre503 and resident director with Equal Measure.

Theatre directing credits include: *Bluebird* by Simon Stephens, *Mr England* by Richard Bean, *Hippolytus* by Euripides (University of Sussex); *Wild East* by April De Angelis (Marlborough, Brighton); *The Poet and the Rent* by David Mamet (Marlborough/Brighton Festival Fringe); *The Sweet Science* by Tinuke Craig, *Bound East for Cardiff/In the Zone* by Eugene O'Neill (LAMDA); *Topdog/Underdog* by Suzan Lori Parks (CounterCulture Project); *Abortive* by Caryl Churchill (The Albany); and *Unmanned* by Laura Stevens (Riverside Studios).

Amy Wildgoose (Assistant Stage Manager)

Amy is a recent graduate of Goldsmiths College, University of London, where she read BA Drama and Theatre Arts. During her time at Goldsmiths, Amy stage-managed various degree performances and captained the university's cheerleading squad.

Babs Iles (Production Assistant)

Recently graduated from Royal Holloway, University of London, with a First-class BA (Hons) degree in Drama and Theatre Studies.

Credits include: *King Lear, The Late Lancashire Witches, Motel, The Merry Wives of Windsor* (Royal Holloway); *Blood Wedding, Whale Music, The Masque of the Red Death*, Seneca's *Oedipus, Cinderella, Playhouse Creatures* (Year Out Drama); *The Two Noble Kinsmen* (Edinburgh Fringe); *Annie, Whistle Down the Wind* (Alhambra, Bradford).

Buckle for Dust
theatre company

Buckle for Dust

Buckle for Dust is a company dedicated to telling stories.

We have a passion for new plays with a twisted take on the everyday world. We believe that stories for the stage should be imaginative, metaphorical and visually brilliant. We fight to create opportunities for distinctive voices.

We are:
Claire Birch
Lou Ramsden
Lisa Spirling
Ali Taylor

Buckle for Dust was formed in 2008, and our first production was *Cotton Wool* by Ali Taylor at Theatre503. The play won the 18th Meyer-Whitworth Award later that year.

'Intelligent writing… thoughtful direction… fantastic performances… demonstrate the wealth of talent available to British Theatre'

The Stage

For more information on the company please see our website:
www.bucklefordust.org.uk, or email us at **info@bucklefordust.org.uk**
You can also follow us on **Twitter** and **Facebook**

Thanks

This production has been made possible by the generous support of:

Arts Council England
Coutts Charitable Trust
Leopold De Rothschild Charitable Trust
Richard Carne Foundation
Royal Victoria Hall Foundation
Split Infinitive

Denise and Keith Birch
Ivailo Bojkov
Mr and Mrs John Deane
Sylvia Goodman
Jennifer and Gaskell Jacobs
Marcus Markou

Radford Wallis
Dynamis

Our special thanks to:

Rachel, Jane, Perri, Marian and all at English Touring Theatre, Steve Marmion and all at Soho, Lolo, Michael and all at the Hospital Club, Jacksons Lane, Gene David Kirk, Steve Mannix, Melanie Sharpe, Barbara Chido, Mark Slaughter, Ben Evans, Graham Birch, Stuart Radford, Andrew Wallis, Talawa Theatre Company, Paula Macintosh, Noel Clerkin, Gary Davy, Adam, Luca, Nancy and all at AKA.

And to all those who helped with this production after this text went to print.

ETT
ENGLISH
TOURING
THEATRE

Photos by: Robert Day, Manual Harlan and Tristram Kenton

surprise • delight • enrich • engage

Under the directorship of Rachel Tackley, ETT presents potent, vivid and vital productions of new and classic plays to audiences far and wide. A powerhouse of touring theatre, ETT works with a rich and varied mix of the country's leading directors, actors and artists to stage thrilling and ambitious theatre that is vigorous, popular and, above all, entertaining.

Producer of the Year 2010

THE STAGE 100 AWARDS

From Edinburgh to Exeter and Sheffield to Southampton – in 2010 we gave 223 performances in 22 venues all over the country – look out for us in your region in 2011!

www.ett.org.uk

 Supported by
ARTS COUNCIL
ENGLAND

 BRITISH
COUNCIL

HUNDREDS AND THOUSANDS

Lou Ramsden

Acknowledgements

Hundreds and Thousands was originally a seed commission for Theatre Absolute. I'd like to say a huge thank you to all those who have given their time and expertise to help develop the play since that point: Chris O'Connell, Julia Negus, Anthony Weigh, Nina Steiger, Giles Smart, Gene David Kirk, Charlie Anson, Lorna Beckett, Alexander Kirk, Dorothy Atkinson, all at The Hospital Club, Monica Dolan, Con O'Neill, Bertie Carvel, Matti Houghton, Dave Hartley, Lacey Turner, and John and Kerry at La Muse writers' retreat. Very special thanks are due to Ali Taylor, Lisa Spirling and Claire Birch.

Lou Ramsden

For Lisa

Characters

LORNA, *forty-three*
JONATHAN, *thirty-nine*
ALLAN, *thirty-seven*
TIGGY, *thirty-two*

Notes

A forward slash (/) suggests an interruption.

A dash (–) at the end of a line indicates that the line feels unfinished.

A dash in place of a line indicates a beat when a character would like to speak, or is expected to speak, but either cannot or will not say anything.

A dash at the beginning of a line indicates that that line connects directly with, or is a continuation of, the same character's previous line.

Music can be used to cover scenes without dialogue and scene changes.

This text went to press before the end of rehearsals and so may differ slightly from the play as performed.

ONE

An evening in late spring. Dying daylight.

The front room of an isolated farmhouse – a little run down, dated, and cluttered.

There is a dining table with chairs, a sideboard, armchairs, one window with thick curtains closed. There is a door into the hall and, to one side, a door that opens onto cellar steps.

Clocks that tick a fusty tick.

LORNA *stands alone, next to a big pile of her boxes. She's moving in.*

LORNA. Self-preservation – that's what it comes down to, I s'pose.

That last stroke he had took his tongue. He couldn't say what he wanted and he was –

Well – scared, that's all. He'd lost control.

She examines a big cut on her arm. She pokes at it.

Me and that nurse, we were trying to make him swallow his pills.

But he got his glass and he brought it down on the edge of that table – such a whack! – didn't know he had it in him!

Shattered it, all sharp, and he jabbed it in my arm –

Tore it through, and it bled like nobody's business.

To be honest, though, I almost didn't mind. I said: 'Let's pretend it never happened. It's okay, because I love you.'

JONATHAN *enters, carrying another box.*

*On top of it he balances his car keys, wallet, and a
newspaper.*

It was only because he was scared. Confused.

JONATHAN. Even so. I think we should write to her.

LORNA. Who, sorry?

JONATHAN. That poor agency nurse. What was her name –
Mercy?

Facing that torrent of abuse every day. (*Dumps the box.*)

LORNA. Does it matter? It's over now.

JONATHAN. If we don't say anything we might as well be
approving of Dad's behaviour.

And I don't want her to think we're that kind of family.

LORNA. He didn't know what he was saying. Some words just
came out –

JONATHAN. 'Some words'?

LORNA. I think she understood that.

JONATHAN. I heard him call her a –

LORNA. A what?

JONATHAN. A – (*Whispering.*) 'nigger', Lorna.

LORNA (*dismissive*). Oh – it's just a word, Jonathan. And
people do use it, sometimes.

JONATHAN. Which people?

LORNA. You know, like –

Rappers.

JONATHAN. I don't think Dad was rapping to her, just then.

Look, I realise that Allan thinks I'm a bit of a bloody namby-
pamby for getting bothered about stuff like this. But I think
it's important / to try and –

LORNA. Yes, yes, I know. (*In* JONATHAN*'s voice.*) 'Speak up.' 'Take action.'

JONATHAN. Is that meant to be me?

LORNA. Last Christmas.

JONATHAN. Jesus, so I *am* a – what was it? – 'tub-thumping tossbag'.

LORNA. He never said that.

JONATHAN. What d'you reckon then? – Write to her or something.

Kate really thinks we should apologise on Dad's behalf.

LORNA (*smiling*). You're right, of course. You're always right.

JONATHAN *is wandering around the room, picking up objects and examining them.*

JONATHAN. Shame Mr Perfect couldn't be here to welcome you himself.

LORNA (*checks her watch*). He'll be back any minute. Just out working the playgrounds.

And I don't know why you're complaining – gives you plenty of time to nosey.

JONATHAN. I'm not noseying.

LORNA. Oh, come on.

JONATHAN. Alright, so the man's got an eye for old crocks.

LORNA. That's no way to talk about your sister.

JONATHAN (*sarcastic*). Ha ha.

You never told me he had such decent stuff.

LORNA. I never knew. Some of it will have to make way for my girls, though.

LORNA *has opened a box and started taking out a collection of porcelain dolls.*

This shelf, I think. (*Shoves a pot along the shelf.*)

JONATHAN. Oi, careful –

He rescues the thing from her. It is a small, round, ivory pot. Carvings of trees or plants.

Blimey, is this – ?

LORNA (*arranging the dolls*). Yes, bit dull, isn't it? Stick it in the cupboard.

JONATHAN. Where did he get it? (*Trying to see it.*) Open the curtains.

LORNA. Why, is it worth something? (*Opens the curtains.*)

JONATHAN (*laughs*). You could say that. Chinese brush pot. Seventeenth century.

And it's – (*Checks the base.*) my God, it's actually signed.

I've seen these at auction fetching / like –

LORNA. Oh, Jonathan, please – please! Don't be vulgar. I don't want to know.

JONATHAN. Won't he?

LORNA. It's probably his mum's. Which means it's best not to dwell. Put it down.

JONATHAN. Beautiful piece.

LORNA. He might let you take it if you're nice to him.

JONATHAN. Oh – God no –

LORNA gives him a suspicious look.

Ivory. Kate won't have it.

But he continues looking at the pot.

LORNA. Oh, well, of course, if *Kate* says…

JONATHAN (*not listening*). Hm?

LORNA tuts, takes the pot from him and puts it down on the sideboard. She gestures to the hallway, where there are more boxes. JONATHAN goes out.

LORNA *surveys the room with a happy sigh.*

LORNA. What d'you think then? In need of a coat of magnolia. Or maybe some nice fresh anaglypta, that'd be sweet.

It's cosy though, isn't it? Just as I imagined, really.

JONATHAN. Imagined?

LORNA. You know. Homely.

JONATHAN. You –

LORNA. And very *Allan*, of course.

JONATHAN. You mean you haven't been here before?

LORNA. Not as such. He wanted it to be a surprise.

JONATHAN. I didn't know you –

God, Lorn, are you sure this is wise?

LORNA. What?

JONATHAN. Moving in. It's only been – what? – six months. And you've never even been to his house?

LORNA. So?

JONATHAN. So don't let him pressure you into this.

LORNA. He hasn't. It was my idea.

We're ready for this.

JONATHAN. Just as long as you're not just doing it because you think you haven't got –

LORNA. Haven't got what?

JONATHAN. Well. Because you haven't got anywhere else to go.

LORNA. That's hardly a nice thing to say.

JONATHAN. I'm sorry. But you know what I mean.

LORNA. I don't, actually.

JONATHAN. Home's sold already. The money from the will is taking so long to come through. *Too* long –

LORNA. I told you, I'll chase them again.

JONATHAN. – and you've not got a lot of friends and stuff since you gave up work.

LORNA. I've got friends. I've got –

JONATHAN. Not counting penfriends.

LORNA. Why are you saying this?

JONATHAN. I worry about you. I care about you. I wish you'd just / think –

He is interrupted by the sound of an ice-cream van pulling up outside, playing a bright tune.

LORNA. God, he's here!

JONATHAN. Please, listen –

LORNA. That's our song! He's playing our song.

Remember – nice to him, this time.

JONATHAN. I'll try. But –

LORNA. Does my hair look okay?

JONATHAN. Lorna, I wish you'd consider moving into ours.

LORNA (*laughs*). No –

JONATHAN. Just for a bit.

LORNA. I'm a grown woman, Jonathan.

JONATHAN. I respect that, but I really do / think –

ALLAN (*offstage*). Where is she then? Where's my little Mini Milk?

LORNA. She's here.

ALLAN (*offstage*). My little Lolly!

ALLAN runs in, grabs LORNA and kisses her passionately.

JONATHAN *hangs back awkwardly.*

JONATHAN. Yeah, I think there's just a couple more boxes in the van, so –

ALLAN (*surprised to see him*). Oh –

LORNA. Sorry, sorry –

Allan, you remember Jonathan.

ALLAN. Right. The little brother.

JONATHAN. Less of the 'little' please. (*Shaking* ALLAN*'s hand*.) How are you, squire?

ALLAN. Good.

No, I'm better than good – I'm absolutely spanking.

Now my girl's where she belongs.

JONATHAN. Yes. And busy, I hear.

LORNA. I'll just – (*Goes out to the hall to fetch a box.*)

ALLAN. Oh, I'm up to my earballs, evenings like this. Can't tear myself away from the little monsters.

JONATHAN. We were just saying –

Too busy to be here to greet her. Which was a shame.

ALLAN. After the spring we've had, I can't turn down the trade.

JONATHAN. Yes, I suppose that's the problem with selling low-value.

You want to raise your stakes, Allan. Take a leaf out of my book.

ALLAN. Ah, yes – how is the junk stall?

LORNA (*returning*). It's a shop, you know that. (*To* JONATHAN.) He knows that.

ALLAN. Oh, a *shop*, is it? – My mistake. How's the junk *shop*?

LORNA. 'Boutique antiquities and curiosities,' we say. It's called The Artique.

ALLAN (*laughs; to* JONATHAN). Thought that up yourself, did you?

LORNA (*proud*). Jonathan did everything himself. Built it up from a backroom of their house.

ALLAN. Then I'll wait with bated breath to hear what's next.

JONATHAN. I'm sorry – ?

ALLAN. Whether you go under.

JONATHAN. –

ALLAN. Lorna told me you'd had a bit of trouble since Christmas. Shame to hear it.

Living off your wife's salary, I suppose.

LORNA. I didn't say it like that.

JONATHAN. Temporarily.

ALLAN. And she doesn't mind that? Having a kept man hanging round.

JONATHAN (*forcing a smile*). Oh, right, I get it.

ALLAN. You know 'liquidation' isn't as sexy as it sounds. Watch her – she'll be off like a shot.

LORNA. Stop it, Allan –

JONATHAN. It's fine, Lorna. I know Allan likes to tease.

And he knows that my wife and I don't believe in either one of us *keeping* the other.

ALLAN. Oh yes, that's what she *says* –

But don't try and tell me she doesn't want to be looked after.

See – (*Hugging* LORNA.) this little lady's the only time I've ever wanted a speed date to slow down, and she won't have to lift a finger from now on. Is this all the stuff then, your highness? Quite an empire.

JONATHAN. Yes, so sorry to have cluttered up your beautiful, pristine lounge.

ALLAN (*to* LORNA). If it's your clutter, I don't mind.

LORNA. Allan did give me a key. Cos I promised not to rummage about till he got here.

JONATHAN. How very trusting.

LORNA. Well – you can't have a marriage without trust, can you?

JONATHAN. What?

ALLAN (*laughing*). Bloody hell.

LORNA. Sorry. Ignore me. Jumping the gun there.

Behind ALLAN*'s back she mouths to* JONATHAN*: 'fingers crossed'.*

ALLAN. Any more boxes?

LORNA. They're heavy –

JONATHAN. I can do heavy, I'll go.

JONATHAN goes. LORNA *hugs* ALLAN.

LORNA. You're so naughty. Baiting him like that.

ALLAN. This is the countryside, Lorn, we like our bloodsports.

What's he doing here anyway? Said you were going to get a taxi.

LORNA. I had to ask. He's got a van.

ALLAN. So have I.

LORNA. His goes faster than ten miles an hour.

ALLAN. But can it play 'Just One Cornetto' *and* 'Greensleeves'?

LORNA (*laughs*). I doubt it.

ALLAN tickles LORNA*, playful.* JONATHAN *returns, struggling in with a heavy box.*

JONATHAN. Blimey, Lorna – (*Chucks the box down.*)

LORNA. Sorry, I just lobbed everything in from the loft.

Oh but don't worry, you'll have some for the shop.

JONATHAN. Unfortunately scratched willow pattern isn't really a top seller at the moment.

Quite like Dad's medals, though.

LORNA. Fine – (*Searches.*) but I want Mum's glass eye –

ALLAN. Jesus.

LORNA (*defensively*). What? It's nice to feel she's watching over me.

(*Rummaging.*) God, so much *stuff*.

JONATHAN. We'll have to divide it fairly. Maybe we could split it into piles according to value and go from / there –

ALLAN. Oh, come on, not now. Lorna must be tired.

JONATHAN. She's fine, she's a tough lady.

ALLAN. But I think she'll need to be taken to bed soon, won't you, love?

LORNA. I'm a bit old to be tucked in.

ALLAN. I don't think so. All day long I been thinking about tucking you.

LORNA (*giggling*). For God's sake – (*To* JONATHAN.) I'm so sorry about him.

JONATHAN. Perhaps later in the week.

LORNA. Make it tomorrow.

ALLAN (*aside, to* LORNA). Can't you go to his?

LORNA. Everything's here now.

ALLAN. Whatever.

(*To* JONATHAN.) Not too early then. We'll need a lie-in.

JONATHAN. Ten o'clock.

LORNA. Perfect.

JONATHAN (*retrieving his keys and wallet*). I'll show myself
out.

ALLAN (*picking up* JONATHAN*'s newspaper, handing it to
him*). Here –

JONATHAN (*doesn't take it*). Lorna reads that too.

JONATHAN *leaves.*

ALLAN *throws the paper on the floor and kicks it under the
sofa. Then scoops* LORNA *up in his arms.*

ALLAN. So. Early night, is it?

LORNA. You're incorrigible!

ALLAN. Haven't seen you for a fortnight.

LORNA. You can see me every day from now on.

ALLAN. I know. How magic is that?

You're amazing, you are. You're clever, and pretty, and –

LORNA. I don't know about that.

ALLAN. – you've got a very nice hairdo today.

LORNA *laughs.*

(*Kisses her.*) Let's go up then. I've set the electric blanket
and everything.

LORNA (*laughs*). Can't we just sit, for a minute? Have tea and
cuddles?

ALLAN. Game of Battleships?

LORNA. No, no, just let me –

Take it all in.

ALLAN *clears a seat for* LORNA *on the battered sofa. She
sits.*

Gentleman-like, he finds a stool and tucks it under her feet.

Feels weird being here. So weird, after I prayed for it for ages.

And, God, it's just *unreal* that Dad's gone.

I was in the garden before – before we left – trying to dig up the little rose we planted over the dog, so I could bring it.

I kept stopping cos I thought I heard him calling for me. Yelling for his cigarettes –

ALLAN (*stroking her hair*). He's gone, love.

LORNA. Hardly feels like it.

Was it the same, when your mum / died?

ALLAN. I don't want to talk about her, Lolly.

LORNA. You can tell *me*, though –

ALLAN. Whatever's done now is done. For both of us. And we got nothing but good times to look forward to. The full works of fun.

LORNA. The full works?

ALLAN. Happiness with sauce *and* a Flake.

She laughs. They kiss again. Then –

The sound of a little tinkling bell behind the cellar door.

ALLAN *ignores it*. LORNA *looks up*.

LORNA. What's that?

ALLAN. Hm?

The bell rings again.

Oh, just Tiggy. Looking for a bit of fuss, I daresay.

Come on, let's go to bed.

LORNA. I'd like to meet Tiggy. Unless she scratches, does she?

ALLAN. Only sometimes.

I was going to wait till morning to introduce you.

LORNA. Stroking them's meant to be relaxing.

ALLAN. I've got something you can stroke / if –

He is interrupted by the bell ringing again, and an imploring look from LORNA.

Fine. I suppose now's as good a time as any.

Closes the curtains, then goes over to the cellar door and unlocks it.

Go on then. Call to her.

LORNA (*calling*). Tiggy!

ALLAN. Louder. She's a bit shy.

LORNA. Tiggy!

The door to the cellar opens. TIGGY *walks out, blinking in the light.*

She is a woman, dressed in filthy home-made clothes.

She has a dog's collar, with bell, round her neck.

Rough farmyard binding twine has been used to tie her wrists and ankles together.

It's just long enough to allow her to move, but short enough to make it difficult.

She stands timidly beside ALLAN, *staring.*

Who's – she?

ALLAN. Tiggy. I said.

LORNA. She's – I thought she was – your cat.

ALLAN. God no. She's much more useful.

And she doesn't make me sneeze.

TWO

About ten minutes later. There are now tea things on the table.

ALLAN *is pouring* LORNA *a cup.* TIGGY *is in the corner, standing shyly.* LORNA *is laughing, spluttering –*

LORNA. No, no, no, I get it. Actually I do *get* it. Because she –

When we were laughing the other day, about – yes –

A beat.

No, I don't get it, actually. I don't get it, Allan.

ALLAN. Get what?

LORNA. Her. The joke.

ALLAN. What's the joke? – I missed it.

LORNA. That she –

ALLAN. She lives here.

LORNA. You *keep* her?

ALLAN. Like I said. Sugar?

LORNA. But she's –

It's –

ALLAN. Hm?

LORNA. Weird, Allan. Isn't it?

A beat. ALLAN *laughs.*

ALLAN. Oh God! – Lorna, you thought –

LORNA (*laughs*). Yes!

ALLAN. I don't *sleep* with her. Blimey, is that what you thought?

No, I told you – she just cleans. Cooks.

LORNA. Right.

ALLAN. Whatever I need. So –

LORNA. So she's like a maid? She's just a maid.

ALLAN. Something like that.

LORNA. But she's wearing a collar. A bell.

ALLAN. So I can keep an ear on her.

LORNA. She came from the cellar.

ALLAN. She likes it down there. Hates windows.

LORNA. And she's tied up.

ALLAN. Oh, not properly, look. Just a gesture. Show her who's boss.

I didn't want her trying any funny business when you were here.

LORNA. 'Funny business'?

ALLAN. She's not used to strangers. I only do what's necessary.

LORNA. Her teeth look bad –

ALLAN. She's a glutton for sweets.

LORNA. Allan, I don't understand. Why have you –

Why does she –

ALLAN. Please, love. Let's not go over it again.

This is just the way it is. The way it's been for years, with our family.

And now you're family too, aren't you?

LORNA *stands, starts trying to gather her stuff.*

LORNA. Except – the thing is –

ALLAN. Hey, what you / doing?

LORNA. I don't know if I can stay here, really.

ALLAN. Course you can. Sit down.

LORNA. No, I think maybe I should go home.

ALLAN. You are home.

LORNA. Yes, but I think perhaps –

ALLAN. You can't go now, sweetheart, don't do that to me.

LORNA. – I should ring Jonathan. Should I?

ALLAN. What? Why?

LORNA. Get him to fetch me –

ALLAN. It's getting late –

LORNA. Can I borrow the / phone?

ALLAN. Be past the kids' bedtime. You don't want to wake them, he'll be cross.

LORNA. I'll – I'll go there then. I'll walk.

ALLAN. It's twenty miles away. It's pitch black, it's not safe. So dark, just at the end of that driveway – you can't see to put one foot in front of the other. And I couldn't bear it, Lorna, if anything happened to you, I –

Please sit down, just for a moment.

LORNA *takes a breath, but doesn't sit*.

Perhaps you'd feel better if she wasn't here.

Out of sight, out of mind? Tiggy, back downstairs now please.

TIGGY *hesitates*.

What's the matter with you? Go on.

TIGGY *approaches him and lifts her hands. She has made her ties into a cat's cradle*.

Come on, Tigs – you know it's not for playing.

(*To* LORNA.) Sorry about this.

LORNA. Playing?

ALLAN (*pulling the string off* TIGGY*'s hands*). I told you, she's a retard.

LORNA. Allan – you can't –

ALLAN (*to* TIGGY). Naughty spot, go on.

LORNA. – you really can't use that word.

TIGGY *sits down in the 'naughty spot'.*

ALLAN. 'Slow', then. 'Special'. Thinks we can go on like when we were kids.

LORNA. Kids? What is she, your sister?

ALLAN (*quickly*). No. Never. No. We only found her.

LORNA. I don't understand –

ALLAN. Round the back of the cowshed out there, where the fly-tippers swarm.

Dumped with all the other unwanted stuff. Mum took her in, dusted her down, named her after the farm cat that'd just died having a litter.

Even when she was a baby we could tell she was a couple of gobstoppers short of the jar. And she's mental still, but she won't bite.

LORNA. You should have told me she was here.

ALLAN. Oh, not till now. We don't tell outsiders, love. Family rules.

Mum didn't want to risk anyone taking her –

TIGGY *cowers at this prospect.* ALLAN *tries to calm her.*

LORNA. Taking her? You mean / into care?

ALLAN (*to* TIGGY, *soothing*). Oh, it's alright, shhh, don't make a fuss.

Go and fetch that – that *thing* in the kitchen, for me.

TIGGY *looks blank.* ALLAN *grabs her to him and whispers.*
TIGGY *nods. She goes out to the kitchen.*

LORNA. But – there must be someone who knows about her.

What about visitors – callers –

ALLAN. Come on, love, you know the way things are. People
mind their own.

LORNA. But when she goes outside –

ALLAN. I told you, she doesn't.

LORNA. What, never?

ALLAN. She's scared of outside. She can't keep it real, up here
– (*Taps his head.*)

LORNA. Because she's a re–

Because she's got learning difficulties?

ALLAN. That's it. See, you're getting it.

(*Kissing her.*) Now, let's forget about her, please, just for
tonight.

Let's pretend she doesn't even exist.

LORNA. I want to. I want to stay with you, Allan –

ALLAN. I knew you would. Thank / God!

LORNA. – but I'm really not sure that I should.

He goes to kiss her again. She takes a step back from him.

He collects himself.

ALLAN. Right. That's your final decision, is it?

It's a shame. I never thought you'd be like this.

LORNA. Like what?

ALLAN. Prejudiced.

LORNA. I'm not / –

ALLAN. Closed-minded. You've always seemed to have 'principles', you and your brother.

LORNA. I have. We have.

ALLAN. I didn't think you'd be so intolerant of other lifestyles.

LORNA. I'm not *intolerant*. If we'd had the chance to – to discuss it before –

ALLAN. My mistake then. I suppose I just wanted you to see for yourself, the way we live, before you started – well, judging us.

LORNA. I'm not judging you –

ALLAN. And maybe I thought you'd see things our way, if you really loved me.

LORNA. What?

ALLAN. But perhaps you don't.

LORNA. Oh God, don't say that. You know I adore you – you've changed my life –

ALLAN. Would have been good to have your help then, to change mine too.

LORNA. Help with what?

ALLAN. You know, that *nurturing* thing, that you do so well.

LORNA. Do I?

ALLAN. Oh, Lorn – you're so caring, sweet, selfless.

None of this foul-mouth you get these days.

LORNA. I try –

ALLAN. You got morals so clean you could eat your dinner off them.

And here she is, in need of a bit of that kind of guidance.

Oh, things were bound to be a bit strange tonight, weren't they?

But you should see her most days. When she's trying to get her own way she'll do anything. Anything for a sweetie.

That day we found her, she'd been abandoned by everyone, you know.

We didn't think you'd abandon her too.

Never mind though.

A beat. He finds LORNA*'s coat.*

Here. Rain on the way.

LORNA. Well, maybe I could –

ALLAN. Hmm?

LORNA. If I could just ask Jonathan what he thinks.

ALLAN. Lorna, she's nobody's business but mine, alright?

And yours now. And I'm going to trust you not to talk about her.

Because – we can't have a marriage without trust, can we?

LORNA. What?

ALLAN. Sorry. Shouldn't have said that. Jumping the gun.

He opens the living-room door for her.

LORNA *doesn't move.* ALLAN *waits.*

Then, TIGGY *arrives at the lounge door. She is carrying a birthday cake, with burning candles.*

Ah, yes. The surprise! Come on in, Tigs.

LORNA (*as* TIGGY *puts the cake in front of her*). Oh! – that's –

I thought everyone had forgotten.

ALLAN. Not me.

LORNA. Forgot myself, really. Or maybe I just didn't want to think about it.

ALLAN. Why? – When you're only that old.

LORNA (*counts the candles*). Eighteen?

ALLAN (*mock surprise*). Is that not right?

LORNA (*allowing herself a smile*). No.

ALLAN. Looks like we messed up again, Tigs.

LORNA. Oh no, thank you. (*To* TIGGY, *slowly.*) Thank. You.

ALLAN. Stay tonight, Lorna. What harm can one night do?

This whole thing will make sense in the morning, I promise.

LORNA. Will it?

ALLAN. Perfect sense. Sleep with me. I mean – on it. Sleep on it.

A short pause, then LORNA *sits down.*

THREE

The next morning. The curtains drawn. Sunshine outside.

TIGGY *is in the front room alone – cleaning, tidying, neatening. Her morning routine.*

LORNA *enters. She looks teary and tired.* TIGGY *hides, shyly, as she comes in.*

LORNA *checks her watch, then picks up one of her packing boxes and puts one of the dolls in.*

Then takes it out. Then puts it in again.

She paces for a second, then goes to the window. Lifts the curtain to look out.

TIGGY. Don't do / that!

LORNA (*surprised*). Oh – shit!

TIGGY (*a new word – to herself*). 'Oh shit'?

LORNA. I'm sorry, excuse my –

You scared me.

I didn't mean to interrupt your – duties, I just –

I wanted to sort out my dolls.

Allan said you like dollies and things too, do you, cos you're – cos –

TIGGY *stares*. LORNA *is uncomfortable under her gaze*.

I thought I might slip away. I hate goodbyes, and he's still sleeping, so –

Look, I'll make sure I tell someone, okay? I'll send help.

And that'll mean your brother –

Well, you might not see him any more, / but –

TIGGY. You're leaving?

LORNA. Oh, I want to stay, so much –

TIGGY. My mum said – 'If you want something, have it.'

LORNA. Yes, well. I'm not sure it always works that way.

A beat. She checks her watch.

It's – it's nearly ten. (*Leaving.*) Jonathan'll be here soon, so –

TIGGY (*blocking her way*). Please – I need to ask you something.

LORNA. It's alright, I'll wait for him / outside –

TIGGY. No, wait – wait!

LORNA *stops*.

I need to know how you did it.

Are you an enchantress? Or a witch?

If I touch you, can I catch it?

She reaches out to touch her. LORNA *backs away*.

LORNA. Erm –

I'm sorry, I don't understand.

TIGGY. He told me that you'd come here by yourself.

LORNA. Well, no. My brother gave me a lift.

TIGGY. So you must have got through the flaying forest, somehow.

Flew all the way here, and they never managed to slaughter you, or take your head.

And all last night, I never slept for the wondering –

About how you got past them.

LORNA (*laughs*). Is this a – ?

Got past who?

TIGGY. You know. The Hatters. The man-hunting monsters.

The ones with the holes for eyes and nails for their cannibal teeth.

LORNA *pauses*.

LORNA. The man-hunting – ?

TIGGY. Yes, exactly.

Oh, it's alright, you don't have to watch your tongue – I know, already.

They hide, outside the house, watching for people to eat. In hunting packs – black uniforms – tall hats. Tall enough to hide your head so once they've sawed it off they can sneak it home to stew. Usually you can only make it safely through if you're locked in the ice-cream van. The magic music scares them away, but *you* –

You made it here without.

LORNA. Well, yes, I must be special.

TIGGY. Why are you laughing?

LORNA. Did Allan put you up to this?

It really is a joke, isn't it? This whole thing –

TIGGY (*firmly*). No! No.

Oh, you poor, ignorant lady. Has no one told you the truth?

Our woods are full of them. The whole farm, infested.

They can run five times as fast as you, on their jaunty spring legs, and if they catch you they'll poke your eyeballs out with their golden spoons and swallow them so quickly you'll glimpse the inside of their belly before you stop seeing. They'll boil the flesh off your skull then turn it on their lathe, smooth it to a ball so they can play ninepins with your bones, in the long corridors of their slaughterhouses.

LORNA. And have you –

Have you seen them, these people?

TIGGY. Shadows, sometimes.

LORNA. Shadows?

TIGGY. Shapes, from the windows.

But I can never, *ever* go outside. Ladies they like more than anything.

LORNA. My God, you really are – (*Shakes her head, surveying* TIGGY *sadly.*)

Poor Allan. And poor you, you strange little –

TIGGY. –

LORNA. Here. Let me help. Let me –

LORNA *opens the curtains and stands in front of the window.* TIGGY *cowers from the light, afraid.*

TIGGY. No! What are you doing?

LORNA. I think you should have a look.

TIGGY. You're not allowed to do that! Mum's rules!

LORNA. There's no one out / there.

TIGGY. They're everywhere! Shut them –

LORNA. In a minute.

TIGGY. But they'll see you, any moment.

LORNA. Really? Well, let's help them along then. (*Throws opens the window.*)

TIGGY (*laughing at the danger of this*). What are you doing?! You're mad!

LORNA. I'm not. Look, I'm fine, aren't I?

TIGGY. It's a trap!

LORNA. Come here –

TIGGY *shakes her head.*

Just one foot in front of the other.

TIGGY. Stop / it!

LORNA. Please, sweetie – (*Holds a hand out to be held.*)

TIGGY. –

Sweetie?

LORNA. Come on, come here.

TIGGY *backs away – but keeps her eyes on* LORNA, *still intrigued.*

A pause. Then – LORNA *has a new idea. She rummages in her handbag and finds a sweet.*

TIGGY'*s eyes light up as she holds it out to her. An outstretched hand.*

She edges closer, approaching like a frightened bird. She snatches the sweet, puts it in her mouth.

As she relaxes a little, LORNA *grabs her by the wrist. She gently pulls her to the window.*

TIGGY. No, no, no! Stop it!

LORNA. Stand here. Shhhhh – (*Pushes* TIGGY*'s arm out of the window.*)

TIGGY. Let me go!

LORNA. Just for a second.

TIGGY (*quieter*). Your fingernails –

LORNA. You'll thank / me.

TIGGY. – you're hurting!

LORNA. I won't let anything hurt you. I promise.

TIGGY *stands, with* LORNA *holding her arm out of the window.*

She breathes, trying to suppress fear. Her eyes are clamped shut, afraid.

Then, slowly, she opens them.

Relaxes, just a little. Moves her fingers around in the breeze.

TIGGY. It's –

LORNA. Safe, see?

TIGGY (*excitement shining through nerves*). It can't be. It's –

LORNA. Peaceful, isn't it?

TIGGY. –

LORNA. It's so –

TIGGY. Sweet.

LORNA (*pleased*). Yes! So what do you say to me?

TIGGY. I don't know.

LORNA (*as to a child*). What do you say?

A beat.

TIGGY. Thank you.

LORNA *beams with pride. An achievement.*

LORNA. There. Good girl.

Where did you get such silly ideas / anyway?

The doorbell rings. TIGGY *panics.* LORNA *looks out of the window.*

TIGGY. They're here! They saw!

LORNA (*looking out*). It's nothing, it's Jonathan.

TIGGY. I shouldn't have done it!

LORNA. Where are you / going?

TIGGY. Big bell means beware! Back downstairs!

LORNA. Tiggy, listen –

But TIGGY *runs into the cellar and slams the door.*

ALLAN *puts his head around the door to make sure the coast is clear, then leads* JONATHAN *in.* ALLAN *is in his dressing gown.*

ALLAN. Here's the lovely lady. She stayed the night after all, see?

JONATHAN. I assumed that was the plan.

ALLAN. And she's looking twice as radiant for it this morning.

JONATHAN. Not sure I want the details, thanks.

ALLAN. We moved your crappy heirlooms upstairs, out the way.

Wait here, eh, and have some birthday cake.

JONATHAN. Birthday – ? (*Realising.*) Oh – shit –

ALLAN. It's okay, I remembered.

Pity is, she says last night she can't stomach it.

How you feeling this morning though? – Worked up an appetite?

LORNA. Erm – yeah, I'm fine.

ALLAN. Stayed up all night, talking.

And she's still here now, isn't she?

He kisses LORNA *again, leaves.*

JONATHAN *waits for him to go, then closes the door behind him.*

LORNA. Jonathan, I –

I need to talk to you about / something –

JONATHAN. Jesus, Lorn, what kind of a man is he?

LORNA. Oh God. You saw her.

JONATHAN. As I was coming up the driveway.

LORNA. I wanted to ask you. Whether it's *definitely* wrong.

JONATHAN. For Christ's sake, I thought you'd know for yourself.

LORNA. But – he says he wants my help / and –

JONATHAN. And he doesn't deserve it. Lorna, he's a bully. And to be honest, I don't think you should stay here a minute longer.

LORNA. You think – ?

JONATHAN. Tell him you're leaving with me.

I won't allow you to stay here.

He sees the box with LORNA*'s one doll packed in it. He puts the rest in there.*

LORNA. You won't 'allow' me?

JONATHAN. No.

LORNA. I don't need your permission –

JONATHAN. I'm sorry – I didn't mean that, I'm sorry.

But look, you made a stupid choice, that's all, taking up with him so quickly.

It's nothing to be ashamed of.

LORNA. Hang on –

JONATHAN. And now it's fine – I'm here, I'll take control.

LORNA. I don't want you to 'take control'. And I'm not stupid
– will you *stop* – ! (*Grabs her dolls from him.*)

JONATHAN. For God's sake, Lorna, don't get all proud about
this now.

LORNA. Proud? Why shouldn't I be? – I went out and got
someone. I did it myself.

JONATHAN. I think it was Kate who found you the speed
dating –

LORNA. And I love him, so much, and –

JONATHAN. And he's a little thug, and a misogynist.

Come on, I realise you're 'attracted' to this bloke – for some
bloody reason unknown to me, actually, but –

Consider things in the long term.

I mean, I know how much you –

A beat.

But isn't it better to have no kids / at all –

LORNA. Don't say / that.

JONATHAN. – than have them with someone like / that?

LORNA (*emphatically, full of fear*). Jonathan, this is my last
chance.

JONATHAN. But do you really want a family with someone
who victimises people like that –

LORNA. Please, shush –

JONATHAN. – just cos they're a bit overweight?

A beat.

LORNA. Overweight – ?

JONATHAN. That woman outside. The rambler –

LORNA. I didn't see her.

JONATHAN. I thought you said you / knew –

LORNA. What happened?

JONATHAN. She was walking past the house just then, rucksack on, boots and cagoule and –

Well, she looked like she was about to faint from heatstroke, actually.

And Allan was just hanging out the back window, howling at her to get off his land.

LORNA. He doesn't like strangers coming close.

JONATHAN. He said, 'Quick march, lard-arse. Your thighs will thank you for it.'

LORNA (*a release; she sniggers*). I'm sorry, I shouldn't laugh.

JONATHAN. God, I know it's not the world's worst crime but –

Well, if he's like this to complete randoms, what names is he going to end up hurling at you?

LORNA. Oh, come on.

JONATHAN. No, you should have seen her, she was hurt. She started blethering about how anyone could comfort-eat – and he said 'Comfort? I got Lorna's tits for that.'

LORNA (*laughs*). He didn't!

JONATHAN. Actually, no, I think he used the phrase 'fun bags'.

LORNA *laughs*.

No respect for women.

LORNA. Jonathan, you're being a bit petty.

You're only saying this cos he was winding you up about being a kept man.

JONATHAN. I'm saying it cos – well – to put it bluntly, you've not got great self-esteem at the best of times.

LORNA. Thank you so much.

JONATHAN. And living with someone like this isn't g
help. Someone aggressive –

LORNA. What, did he touch her?

JONATHAN. Of course he didn't, but –

LORNA. There, then.

JONATHAN. – but you didn't hear the tone of his voice.

LORNA. Well – like I said. Maybe that's something I could
help him with, now I'm here.

JONATHAN *laughs*.

No, seriously. Perhaps I've been sent here to make things
better.

JONATHAN. 'Sent'? You're not the bloody Messiah, Lorna.

No one's going to change him.

LORNA. But perhaps if I had more time, I could.

I realise he's a bit of a grump, sometimes. But there's a kind
person, underneath – I know it.

Cos he's taken me in, here, when I had nowhere else –

JONATHAN. I told you, stay with / us –

LORNA. – he makes me laugh, just when I'd forgotten what
that felt like.

He makes me feel sexy, and smart, and – *young*.

And he'd be lovely to you too if you'd just let him.

Bet he'd give you that jar you liked for nothing.

JONATHAN. What?

LORNA. That little thing. You said it was worth something.

JONATHAN. I don't care. I don't want it.

LORNA. It's okay to say that you / do.

JONATHAN. No –

LORNA. If you need the money, / you could –

JONATHAN (*louder*). I don't want it! I can't – (*Checks himself.*)

Lorna, this isn't about the stupid pot. I'm here for you.

LORNA. And you still will be in a couple of weeks, won't you?

So what if I just took a fortnight – just to quietly, calmly, make some changes –

JONATHAN. Please –

LORNA. Then perhaps everyone'll be okay.

JONATHAN. You won't be able to change things.

LORNA. Actually, I think I already have. Just a little.

JONATHAN. Oh, you have, have you? How?

ALLAN *returns with one of* LORNA*'s boxes from her dad's.*

ALLAN. Here you go – the family treasures.

Bit tatty, eh. But hey – at least your missus will stick around if her shelves are still getting filled. Ooh, that –

JONATHAN. Kate would not leave me –

ALLAN (*laughs*). – that sounded sort of rude, didn't it?

LORNA (*laughs*). Sort of.

ALLAN (*to* JONATHAN). And look, if you've taken a shine to one of Mum's little pots, you can have it. Flog it.

JONATHAN. What?

LORNA. That's so kind, Allan.

JONATHAN. I didn't tell / you that.

ALLAN. Anything to help you out, eh? Just give me a tenner for it.

JONATHAN. Erm, no – no, thank you. Out of the question.

It's ivory. I don't sell ivory. Or fur. Or golliwogs –

ALLAN. What's wrong with a golly?

JONATHAN. I have an ethical-trading policy in the shop. I won't endorse cruelty.

ALLAN. Well. Your loss.

A beat of tension.

LORNA. Tea! We haven't even offered you tea. And cake –

Walks over to the birthday cake. Takes a knife and cuts a delicate slice.

ALLAN (*excited*). Hang about – you're going to have some?

LORNA. Maybe. Just a small bit though, for now.

ALLAN. Having a small bit's better than having no bits at all.

Oh! – That sounded rude again, didn't it?

LORNA (*giggles*). You're on fire today, you.

ALLAN. Hey – here, let me test it first.

LORNA. I'm sure it'll be fine –

ALLAN. Down the hatch, go on – (*Opens his mouth.*)

LORNA (*to* JONATHAN). Everything will be completely fine, I know it.

LORNA giggles as ALLAN *eats the cake off her fingertips.*

FOUR

A fortnight later. A warm evening.

LORNA *is sitting at the dinner table, wearing her best dress.*
ALLAN *is wearing a tatty tux.*

*They've just finished a meal. They might be wearing children's
party hats.*

*There is a posy of flowers on the sideboard. A gramophone, just
finishing a crackling old tune.*

On the table a small bell, for calling TIGGY.

LORNA *is holding up a picture – a drawing done by* TIGGY.
She points –

LORNA. Think that's you, with the – with the little paunch.
    Sorry.

    And there's me. With the glow.

    Only pencil but it's quite grown up, isn't it? I was expecting
    her to do stick men.

ALLAN. Put it away, love, please.

LORNA. The literacy is coming on as well. (*Holding up
    another piece of paper.*) The other day we wrote a little poem
    about 'Why we should always tell the truth'.

    *He takes the paper from her and screws it up. Then paces,
    uncomfortable.*

    What's the matter? You seem nervous.

ALLAN. Not me. Don't do nervous.

    Just can't get comfy in this get-up. Feel like a right penis.

LORNA. Well, you look like James Bond.

ALLAN. Does he get his suits in the Oxfam as well?

LORNA *laughs*.

Need you to have a nice evening, that's all.

LORNA. I will if you cheer up. Love that schoolboy smile of
yours.

ALLAN. Yeah?

Here it comes, then. Brace yourself.

He grins, deliberately. She laughs.

He relaxes slightly. He remembers –

Oh – erm – (*Grabs the flowers from the sideboard.*) these are
for you.

I love you, Lorna. A lot.

Top trumps, you are.

(*A deep breath, then he rings the bell.*) Time for afters then?

LORNA. Oh, honestly, I couldn't.

ALLAN. Come on, it's all ready. I dare you.

LORNA. In a minute, maybe.

ALLAN. Ah no! – Now I've dared you, you've got to. That's
the rules.

(*Calling.*) Tiggy!

LORNA. Listen, if we're talking about Tiggy again –

ALLAN. Please, let's not.

LORNA. I've been thinking, the last week –

ALLAN (*calling*). Oi! Afters!

LORNA. Perhaps we could all go out together some time.

A beat. ALLAN *laughs*.

ALLAN. Go out?

LORNA. Yes, you know. Have some fresh air. Some fun.

ALLAN. I don't think so.

LORNA. Oh, don't worry – we don't have to tell anyone about her.

But I've got a plan, Allan. I think you'll like it.

See we make her *normal*. Like you said, I'll help her understand things –

ALLAN. You don't get it, love.

LORNA. Get her used to sunlight. To people. And then –

ALLAN. Christ, what's she playing at?

LORNA. – then we find her her own place, somewhere nearby.

ALLAN. She can't go out, love. She can't have 'fun'.

LORNA. Why / not?

ALLAN (*louder*). No, Lorn! She's –

She's got to pay, alright?

A beat. ALLAN *takes a breath to calm himself.* LORNA *laughs.*

I'm sorry, sweetheart, I didn't mean to shout.

LORNA. Pay? What for?

ALLAN. Let's leave it now, okay?

LORNA (*laughs*). But –

ALLAN. She doesn't want to go outside anyway, I told you that. Nightmares.

LORNA. Yes, last week she was having some kind of hallucination – men in hats –

ALLAN (*smiles*). I know.

LORNA. Hellish things stuck in her head –

ALLAN. Stuck, exactly. Glued. It's good, isn't it?

LORNA. –

Good?

ALLAN. Mum was so clever. Knew how to keep her where she needed.

LORNA. Your *mum* told her all that stuff?

ALLAN. And I might have added a couple of details, the last few years.

(*Giggling*.) Just play along, Lorna, won't you? It's funny sometimes.

(*Hearing* TIGGY *approaching*.) Oh – watch –

TIGGY *knocks and enters. She is carrying two sundae glasses full of ice cream.*

Ah, yes. Put them down here, then. (*To* LORNA.) That one's for you.

(*As* TIGGY *turns back to the cellar*.) Oh, and Tigs, a little thought before you go.

Lorna thinks you'd like to go outside.

TIGGY. –

ALLAN. Go wandering in the woods, on your own.

With not so much as a breadcrumb to your name, and no protection from me.

Would you like that?

LORNA (*quietly*). Allan, don't be / daft, now.

ALLAN. Or would you be scared of you-know-who?

What is it that they look like, the Hatters?

TIGGY. They've – (*Looks to* LORNA.)

ALLAN. Go on.

TIGGY (*automatically*). They've got holes for eyes and nails for their cannibal teeth, and tall black hats to hide your head in.

ALLAN. That's right. And what do they want to do?

TIGGY. Saw off your nut and suck your guts up through you like a straw. Cut open your tummy and fill it chock-full of rocks so you can't run away.

ALLAN. Excellent. Remember that, Tigs.

TIGGY. Yes. Except –

ALLAN. That'll be all, thank you.

TIGGY (*looks at* LORNA). Except I thought –

ALLAN. Hm?

You thought / what?

LORNA. Maybe you should go back downstairs now, / Tiggy.

ALLAN. No, you thought what? (*Catching the glance between them.*) What's going on?

TIGGY (*to* LORNA). I thought there was nothing outside.

(*To* ALLAN.) There's nothing to hurt me, she said.

A beat. ALLAN *takes a deep breath, trying to contain himself.*

Is it true?

LORNA. Allan – I didn't know –

ALLAN. Right.

LORNA. I hope I haven't messed up. I just didn't / know –

ALLAN. Oh, Lorna, don't look so worried. Not your fault.

LORNA. Okay.

(*Smiling.*) And it is a bit silly, isn't it?

TIGGY. Is it true then?

ALLAN (*to* LORNA). Just give me a minute, love, will you?

ALLAN *pulls* TIGGY *to one side. He talks quietly to her.*

TIGGY. Cos, I've been thinking –

ALLAN. Course it's not true, alright?

TIGGY. She said it though. And I've been / thinking –

ALLAN. Tiggy, shush.

TIGGY. – if it is, I could go outside and see Mum. You never told me where you took her.

ALLAN. She's dead, she's nowhere.

LORNA (*peering over*). What are you two talking / about?

TIGGY. But *she* said 'Green Lawns', yesterday.

LORNA. Do you want me to come over?

ALLAN (*to* LORNA). No, no. Just have a seat.

TIGGY (*to* ALLAN). Where's Green Lawns?

ALLAN. It doesn't matter – there's Hatters out there – you can't go.

TIGGY. No / but –

ALLAN. We'll talk about this later. (*Turning from* TIGGY.)

TIGGY. – no, but she let me look – I put my hand out!

ALLAN stares at TIGGY, *a beat of shock at her rebellion.*

LORNA. Remember then, Allan. *Smile*. For me?

Still numbed by surprise, ALLAN *looks up at* LORNA. *She does the 'schoolboy smile'. He copies, forcing a grin.*

LORNA sits down with her back to them and starts eating the ice cream.

ALLAN (*to* TIGGY, *quietly, still trying to smile*). You did what?

TIGGY (*whispers excitedly*). I put my hand, through the window. I scratched the sunshine! The sky breathed on me! It felt so sweet!

And there was no Hatters – I think they've gone / away!

ALLAN. You broke Mum's rules? You touched outside –

TIGGY. Only for a second.

ALLAN. You know that's not allowed! And –

(*A glance to* LORNA. *Quietly.*) – and you know what we have to do now.

TIGGY*recoils, shakes her head.*

ALLAN *nods.*

TIGGY *looks to* LORNA – *'What about her?'*

LORNA (*her back to them*). This ice cream, love. Delicious. What is it, raspberry ripple?

ALLAN (*to* LORNA). I'm glad you like it. Take your time then.

In silence, behind LORNA'*s back,* ALLAN *and* TIGGY *begin a controlled and well-practised ritual.*

He goes to the sideboard and searches in the drawer.

He produces a pair of pliers and shows them to TIGGY. *She shrinks back.*

He beckons her. She shakes her head. Meanwhile, with her back to them, LORNA *eats and talks…*

LORNA. You really are naughty though, spoiling me like this.

ALLAN (*talking to* LORNA, *looking at* TIGGY). You deserve it.

LORNA. Is – is everything okay over there?

ALLAN (*smiling*). Everything's just fine, love. Enjoy your ice cream.

ALLAN *points to the flat surface of the sideboard.*

Slowly, scared, TIGGY *goes to him and places her hand down in front of him.*

ALLAN *gives her something to bite down on. Then closes in on her fingers, with the pliers.*

All this as LORNA *continues to chatter, just a little uncomfortable now…*

LORNA. Hundreds and thousands as well! How did you know I loved those?

They make everything look more pretty. My mum used to stick them on little cakes for us – even when she was poorly she still made the effort with that kind of thing. Jonathan called them 'fairy sneezes' – he was always stupid like that.

I remember the last birthday we had with her she said – 'Every one of those little specks –

ALLAN *readies himself to pull out one of* TIGGY*'s nails with the pliers.*

– Every one is a kiss I'll leave behind for you.'

ALLAN (*to* TIGGY). Ready? (*Grips her nail.*)

TIGGY *gives a tiny squeal, bracing herself for pain.*

(*To* TIGGY, *quietly*). Steady. (*Grips the pliers.*)

LORNA (*hearing* TIGGY, *she half-turns to object*). Allan, look, what are / you – ? (*Then stops as she sees something in her ice cream.*) My God – (*Fishing it out.*)

ALLAN. Now – (*About to pull.*)

LORNA (*louder*). Oh God! How – beautiful!

LORNA*'s voice cuts through the room and stops* ALLAN *in his tracks.*

From the bottom of her sundae glass, she has fished out a diamond engagement ring.

She holds it up to the light, amazed.

You – you hid it in my – !

ALLAN *looks up, lets* TIGGY *go.* LORNA *turns to him, as he quickly hides the pliers in his pocket.*

ALLAN. Erm – yeah. Yeah, that was my idea. Like a Screwball, remember them?

Except I thought – what's even better than bubblegum?

(*Nervous*.) Will – will you then?

LORNA *looks to* TIGGY.

(*Worried*.) What's the matter?

LORNA. You promise everything's – ?

ALLAN. Oh, fine. Of course it is.

And it will be, for ever, if you just say yes.

Cos I think we need each other, Lolly, don't we?

I ticked you and you ticked me. And two ticks means we're twice as right.

Two ticks means I won a prize that night, didn't it? I won you.

LORNA *nods, smiles*.

Go on then. Marry me. I dare you.

LORNA *laughs. A flicker of hesitation as she looks to* TIGGY *again, then –*

She puts the ring on. ALLAN *is over the moon.*

You will – of course you will. It's proper now.

FIVE

A couple of weeks later. A dark and muggy morning. The curtains closed.

On the sideboard, the posy that ALLAN *presented to* LORNA. *It is shoved in the pot which* JONATHAN *admired, wilting now in the oppressive heat.*

TIGGY *is in the lounge, cleaning and dusting. But this time she moves more slowly. In pain.*

And the twine used to bind her wrist has now been replac
crudely adapted bicycle chains.

As she's cleaning, she notices something sticking out from under
the sofa.

She pulls it out and we recognise it as the newspaper ALLAN
discarded in Scene One.

She opens it. Looks at the pictures. Runs her fingers over them.

There are people. Smiling faces. And TIGGY *smiles too.*

She carries it from the room.

As TIGGY *leaves, lights up on another part of the stage. A day*
or so later.

We see LORNA *enter with a box of her stuff from home, still to*
be sorted.

She puts it down and rummages in it, looking for a tin of crayons.

She finds them, puts them on the table.

Then, in the box, she spots something she didn't expect to – a
jar. She holds it up, pleased.

We see it contains a glass eye – her mum's. She tips the jar so
that it rolls inside.

Then takes the eye out and makes it look at her. Wink at her.

She puts the jar aside and goes out, carrying the eye.

ꞵ days later.

TIGGY *is sᵢ.. ng at the table. She is using* LORNA*'s crayons to do colouring, as* LORNA *watches over her.*

Her wrists are still chained and she moves them in pain.

LORNA *sees this, and* TIGGY *catches a fleeting moment of guilt pass her face.*

She takes advantage of this to ask to be unlocked – holds her wrists out to LORNA*, imploring.*

LORNA *shakes her head.* TIGGY *turns back to the colouring, a little sulkier. A pause.*

TIGGY. He never did so much of the ouch game, before you came.

LORNA. Well – well, perhaps if you learned to stick up for yourself a little more –

LORNA *trails off. She hovers at* TIGGY*'s shoulder, looking at her drawing. Points, encouragingly.*

Oh, that's – that's *very* good. And who's that chap, there?

TIGGY. Mummy.

LORNA. Ah. Sorry. Allan said she had long hair, so –

TIGGY. And that's me. In her special room.

I'm saying her a story, there. Off my heart. Her favourite was *Rapunzel*.

When I was small, I told tales that took her somewhere else. And for every 'happily ever after' she let me have an ice cream from the old freezer. He couldn't stop me then – I could open its cold tummy and have whatever I wanted.

LORNA. That's nice.

TIGGY. Yes. And now I want –

LORNA (*sorting through pencils*). What? – A bit of grey to do her hair?

TIGGY. No. You know.

LORNA. Yellow then, for her dress? Yellow's my / favourite.

TIGGY. I want to go and see Mum. Go out beyond the wood.

'Green Lawns', like you said.

A beat.

LORNA. You – you can't.

TIGGY. But you said, take flowers to her. Then it'll stop – that ache I got in my middle –

LORNA. I shouldn't have encouraged you. You know why.

TIGGY. It's okay outside, though. I know it. I've felt it.

Let me go.

LORNA. One day. Patience.

TIGGY. No, not 'one day' –

LORNA. If we're just a little patient we can all have what we / want.

TIGGY. No! Now! (*Stamps her foot*)

LORNA (*laughs*). I beg your pardon?

TIGGY. I want it now.

LORNA. You know that Brother won't allow it. And I've promised him –

Do you know 'promise'? – (*Grabs the paper and writes it.*)

TIGGY (*screwing up the paper*). I'm not asking him. I'm asking you. When he's out, tonight.

A beat. Then ALLAN *enters, agitated.*

ALLAN. The tossbag has arrived. Didn't I tell him to – (*Stops as he sees* TIGGY.)

Why's she out?

LORNA. We're just – we're having a little lesson.

ALLAN. I thought we agreed. We only let her up here now when we need her to work –

The doorbell rings.

LORNA. What does he want?

ALLAN. Fuck knows. (*To* TIGGY.) Well, what are you waiting for? (*Points to the cellar.*)

(*To* LORNA.) And make sure the door's locked.

LORNA (*approaching him*). I will if you give me a kiss.

ALLAN (*giving her a peck, then backing away*). I'll keep him in the porch. Get on with it.

ALLAN *goes out.* LORNA *looks surprised and disturbed by this new rejection.*

LORNA *finds a bunch of keys in her pocket, goes to the cellar door, opens it.*

As her back is turned, TIGGY *goes to the window and lifts the curtain the tiniest fraction.*

Still timid, but a little braver. She drops it back quickly as LORNA *turns to her.*

LORNA. Tiggy!

TIGGY *goes into the cellar.* LORNA *locks the door behind her then hurriedly tidies the room.*

ALLAN *returns, leading* JONATHAN *in. He looks tired and anxious.*

Jonathan. Wasn't expecting you today.

JONATHAN. Yes, I know you said to ring ahead, but there's –

There's something I needed to – erm – (*Looks to* ALLAN, *uncomfortable…*)

LORNA. Oh, it's alright, I know why you're itching to see us.

JONATHAN. Do you?

LORNA (*showing him her engagement ring*). You can ask to see. Allan won't think you're a big gay cos you want to clock the rock.

JONATHAN. Ah. Yes, sparkly.

LORNA. And a bit sticky, even now. It was a Screwball proposal.

JONATHAN. Congratulations.

ALLAN. He said he's brought us a present.

JONATHAN. Sort of. It's –

ALLAN. Late, but whatever.

LORNA. Never mind. Never too late for presents. Can I – ? (*Takes the bag from him.*)

JONATHAN. I hope you won't think it's odd. It's just a few bits. But –

Having a few bits is better than having no bits at all, eh, Allan?

A lame laugh.

LORNA (*takes out a rattle*). Oh – sweet! (*And a couple of baby toys.*)

ALLAN. What the hell – ?

JONATHAN. Ah, not just any old tat.

That's handmade. And the little teddy is organic cotton.

They were for our two, of course, but they've outgrown them now.

I was going to just chuck them, but then Lorna rang with the news, so I thought –

ALLAN. We're engaged, that's all.

JONATHAN. Oh, it's fine – you don't have to say anything. Early doors, I realise.

Let's just say, she dropped some hints.

LORNA. Did I?

JONATHAN. And I wanted to share in the initial excitement.

ALLAN. She shouldn't have dropped hints.

LORNA. I didn't mean to.

JONATHAN. Sorry, no. But you are – ?

I thought that's why you were –

(*Sees their faces, a beat.*) Oh God. I got the wrong end of the stick.

ALLAN. There is no 'stick'.

LORNA. Not yet, you see, but –

JONATHAN. I'm so sorry. I'll take these back.

LORNA. No – no – please don't.

JONATHAN. I'm sorry, Allan.

LORNA. We can just keep them in storage or something, can't we?

JONATHAN. I suppose you could.

ALLAN. Why would we – ?

JONATHAN. Until you do need / them.

ALLAN. No, but I'm not sure we ever will. Thanks all the same.

A beat.

LORNA. Allan, stop that.

ALLAN. Stop what?

LORNA (*to* JONATHAN). He's such a hoot, this one.

ALLAN. I'm not – hooting, love. No point keeping what we'll never need.

LORNA. Whyever not? A baby, Allan –

ALLAN. I know what they're for.

LORNA. There, then. And you said you wanted kids.

ALLAN. Never said anything of the sort.

LORNA. Well. Maybe not out loud, but –

You're an ice-cream man. You're great with children.

I thought you'd want some of your own.

ALLAN. Maybe. Some time, I don't know.

LORNA. There you go.

ALLAN. But it's not that simple, is it? We've – (*Eyeing* JONATHAN.)

We've got a lot on our plate as it is.

LORNA. Like what?

ALLAN. Let's talk about it later, / sweetheart.

LORNA. No, no, now's as good a time as any.

Go on. What could we possibly have 'on our plate'?

ALLAN. One very big responsibility already. You know that, Lolly.

A beat.

LORNA (*laughs*). You're not serious.

ALLAN (*to* JONATHAN). This house. Maintenance. Old places are expensive.

(*To* LORNA.) We haven't got the time or the money for anyone else.

LORNA. Then, for God's sake, let's get rid of it – this 'big responsibility'.

ALLAN. Lorn, we've had that conversation –

LORNA. Let it / go –

ALLAN. No! That topic's closed.

LORNA. But you don't seem to understand, Allan.

(*A little panicked*.) I *have* to have –

I mean, surely you want to have – something that's only your own, like that?

To build yourself, but better. Start the future.

Don't you have that sort of – furious ache – in the middle of you? All day and night.

You must have something you want that much.

ALLAN. Course I do.

LORNA. Well, then / –

ALLAN. *You*, Lolly.

D'you know?

A beat.

LORNA (*smiles*). I do, love, yes. So –

Say you'll think about it. For me.

ALLAN (*retreating*). Fine. Some time.

LORNA (*laughs*). – I might not have 'some time'.

JONATHAN. Allan, before you go –

– *but he has left*.

An awkward pause.

Oh dear.

Can of worms there. My fault. I'm so sorry.

God and this was meant to be –

Well, an apology, actually. A peace offering.

You will tell him, won't you? I was only trying to –

LORNA. Yes, yes.

JONATHAN. I just wanted to show some – generosity –

He glances to the ivory pot he admired.

LORNA. May be best if you went now, though.

I need some time to think.

JONATHAN. Oh – erm –

In a minute, maybe. I don't want to leave you upset.

LORNA. Jonathan –

JONATHAN. No, you think away. Don't mind me.

She turns from him. He takes advantage of this to touch the ivory pot.

Removes the flowers from it, shakes the water off, and puts them on the sideboard.

A pause.

He – erm –

He did make one very good point, though, you know.

Kids *can* be such a financial drain.

It's one thing after another, I'll tell you – clothes, shoes, books, school trips –

As he chats, LORNA *is pulling out more things from the bag. Another toy. A baby monitor.*

She turns it off and on, off and on, lost in thought.

– God and the food. They eat like – like camels or something, Lorna.

Chomp their way through your bank account, Pacman-style. And that really does put pressure on everything else, you see?

Relationship. Business.

Do you know what I'm – ?

LORNA. We could manage.

JONATHAN. No, no, but I'm talking about serious money.

Real, serious –

And would you really want to be in that position?

Do you want to have to be taking out silly loans and things? Like – like I've had to.

A beat. He waits for a response from LORNA. *It doesn't come.*

I mean, I should say – in my defence – I did apply to the bank. Turned me down twice, the fuckers.

So I had to be proactive. And I was, I found an alternative. I found this – man.

Friend of a friend.

Oh, very nice, first time we met, bought me a Guinness and he's all smiles.

But of course that's changed now. Now it's just 'ten days – you've got ten days or – '

And you don't need that, Lorn. The strain it puts on a marriage.

Cos let me tell you, it's not nice – that moment when Kate says –

'It's just a shop. Let it go.'

And I'm about to agree, you know, but then – I see it. A look.

A look on her face, like utter disappointment. Pity. Shame, even.

And then I remember what Allan said about –

And I think – what if he's right? I mean, I know that's stupid, but I suddenly can't stop myself from thinking what if she – what if she really did –

Panic bubbles to the surface. A deep breath to steady himself.

I'm sorry.

Lorna, I'm so sorry to do this, when you've got your own stuff to think about.

And I wouldn't dream of asking if I wasn't running out of time with this.

Are you listening?

LORNA. Running out of time.

JONATHAN. You can see where I'm coming from, I hope.

LORNA. Precisely.

JONATHAN. I've tried everything else. Asked that solicitor to release the money from Dad's will, but he's stalling again. You know what it's like when you've asked and asked –

LORNA. And you get nowhere.

JONATHAN. And eventually you just think –

LORNA. I can't ask him any more. You're right.

JONATHAN. – I've got to stop talking and *do something*.

LORNA. Even if it's something that you swore you wouldn't do?

JONATHAN. Maybe so, yes. Cos we all have to do things we're not proud of, sometimes.

And I suppose we just have to remember that –

He picks up the pot. She is staring at the cellar door.

That if you're doing that thing for the right reason, then it can't be wrong. Can it?

LORNA. No. You're right, of course.

You're always right.

He pulls a ten-pound note from his pocket. Puts it in place of the pot.

SEVEN

Evening, the same day. ALLAN *is getting ready to go out, combing his hair in the mirror.*

LORNA *is wearing her dressing gown and slippers. Silence, as he preens.*

LORNA. You did that side already.

Aren't you going to be late?

ALLAN. I've got ages. There's races on all night.

LORNA. Thought you'd be meeting friends beforehand, or something.

ALLAN. Don't be daft, Lolly, I haven't got any friends. Told you that.

No one in my class had a train set to match yours truly – and if they thought they were sharing mine, they had another think coming.

(*Turning to show her his hair.*) Well?

LORNA. A frog into a prince.

ALLAN. Oi! Hotter than a May bank holiday, me.

Pass my jacket.

She does. He is ready to go.

LORNA. Good luck, then. Pick some top dogs.

ALLAN. And you're going to – what? – go to bed?

LORNA. One of my headaches coming on. Think you wear me out.

ALLAN. All part of the service.

Oh, and – (*From his back pocket, he takes the baby monitor* JONATHAN *brought. Gives it to* LORNA.) Listen out for trouble, remember? Might else well use it as bin it.

They stand at the doorway together. A beat. Waiting.

Lights?

LORNA. Oh – yes – (*Turns the light off.*)

He kisses her and leaves, as she turns to head for bed.

We hear the front door close behind him.

Then the sound of his van, driving away, as LORNA *scurries back into the darkened living room.*

She goes to the window to watch him drive off. Rain begins outside.

LORNA *stands, looking at the baby monitor for a moment. Then –*

Turns back into the room, puts the monitor down, and fumbles nervously for her bunch of keys.

When she's sure the coast is clear, she goes to the cellar door and unlocks it.

She runs down a few steps and returns, dragging TIGGY.

It's time, come on.

TIGGY. You said you'd get me flowers for her.

LORNA. What? – Oh, here – (*Gives her the dead flowers* JONATHAN *placed on the sideboard.*)

I'll unlock the front.

TIGGY. I'm going to go to Green Lawns. I really am. Then to – everywhere.

LORNA. Get your coat on, it's raining.

TIGGY *looks blankly.*

God's sake –

She takes her own coat and throws it to her.

LORNA *goes out into the hallway. Unlocks and opens the front door.*

TIGGY *goes to the doorway of the living room, where she can see the open door.*

At the sight of it she cowers back with new uncertainty. Backs away and heads for the cellar.

If you run now you'll be able to get as far as – (*Sees her leaving.*) – Hey! – Hey, wait – what you doing?

She grabs TIGGY.

TIGGY. I've changed my mind. It's going dark.

LORNA. So?

TIGGY. I won't see them in the black. The Hatters.

LORNA. Christ, I told you, that's all made / up –

TIGGY. They'll butcher / me!

LORNA. – and you said you believed me.

TIGGY. I did. Now I'm scared. Oh shit.

LORNA. Oi, watch your mouth –

TIGGY. Oh shit.

LORNA. You still want to see her, don't you?

'If you want something, have it.'

TIGGY. Mum said –

LORNA. Yes. So you have to be brave.

TIGGY. Brave. Oh shit.

As she undoes TIGGY*'s wrist chains...*

You as well. Brother will be angry, won't he?

LORNA. For a bit. Maybe. But I'll bear it – for you, Tiggy.

So what do you say?

TIGGY. Thank you.

LORNA. There.

Now you remember what we agreed.

TIGGY. 'Go to the big road and run.'

LORNA. Which way?

TIGGY (*indicating 'right'*). Follow the hand that does colouring.

LORNA (*prompting*). And run as fast as – ?

TIGGY. As a woodcutter after a wolf.

LORNA (*bending to undo her ankle chains*). Good. And if people say:

'Where do you come from, girl?'

TIGGY. 'I don't remember.'

LORNA. 'Who is your family?'

TIGGY. 'Fuck knows.'

LORNA. It's 'I don't know.' Tiggy, you have to promise to get it right.

TIGGY (*rehearsing the line*). 'I don't know.'

LORNA. – or I won't do this, okay?

TIGGY. I promise, I promise.

I'll run, won't I? Spin my legs under me. I've been dreaming what that feels like.

I'll dart through the hunting forest. Dance cos there's no one to catch me. Dash all the way through the town and out the other side and find Mum, sleeping. (*Takes a piece of paper from her pocket, and reads with difficulty.*) Row three. Plot seventeen.

LORNA. Keep still –

TIGGY. I'll put these – (*The flowers*.) down with her and finish the last story – the one where she died before 'happily ever'. And then I'll get an ice cream again. Two, three, four, five, six ice creams. And they'll taste even better than they ever tasted.

LORNA. I said keep still –

LORNA is still crouched, fiddling with the locks, which are stiff now.

Neither of them notice ALLAN walk silently to the darkened doorway. He is wet from the rain. He watches them.

TIGGY. And I'll get some 'friends'. And talk to them, and make them all mine like Mum, and together we'll run and run and run so far and so fast that Brother won't never be able to find me ever / again cos –

ALLAN. Heavens opened.

He flicks the lights on. LORNA and TIGGY freeze.

Suddenly. Downpour.

Should have felt it coming, but I never did.

And then I thought – must be a sign that I should come back.

Cos I had something to say to you, Lorna.

And I couldn't wait to tell you, cos you're my special – beautiful –

A faint flicker of pain across ALLAN's face –

– which is dismissed as he notices TIGGY trying to back away quietly.

Oh, Tiggy – before you go back down, I wondered –

She stops.

Why are you wearing a coat?

TIGGY (*tries to look to LORNA*). I – don't –

ALLAN. What's the matter?

TIGGY. I don't know.

ALLAN. Well, it's a simple question, dumbo.

You don't have a coat. You don't need a coat, do you?

TIGGY. No.

ALLAN. So whose is it?

LORNA. It's mine.

ALLAN. Yours? Ah, yes, I recognise it now. So why is she – ?

LORNA. It's – cold in here.

ALLAN. No. No, it's not cold in here, sweetheart.

LORNA. All of a sudden –

ALLAN. Yes, all of a sudden it's really raging hot in here, I think.

So why is she wearing a coat?

LORNA. Smile, Allan –

ALLAN. Of course. Just as soon as you've told me the truth.

TIGGY. She will – she said you always got to.

ALLAN. Let's hear it then.

TIGGY. She's going to let me go. On my own.

ALLAN. Oh, no, she wouldn't do that.

TIGGY. Yes, she is. Run around. Have friends. (*To* LORNA.) Tell him –

ALLAN. Come on then. I'm listening.

LORNA *opens her mouth to speak, but nothing comes out.*

Ah, see this is sad, Lolly. What we've got here.

I thought us two would be happily ever after.

LORNA. Course – course we / will –

ALLAN. I thought we'd be young together, Lorn – well, young-*ish*. Having fun.

Then grow old surrounded by children and sweet sweet grandchildren with adoring faces, bringing baskets to our house in the / woods –

LORNA. Children – ?

ALLAN. Yes. Can't you imagine?

LORNA. But you said –

ALLAN. Oh, I know, I know I *said*. But people can change their minds, can't they? I can.

LORNA. You –

You can?

ALLAN. Of course. I just did.

I was heading onto the road, just now, and like I said it started raining, and that's when I thought –

How much better it would be to be inside, on a night like this.

Calm and cosy, with people who'll keep your heart dry.

LORNA (*excited*). Yes, exactly. Yes!

ALLAN. Exactly. And I just had to stop the van then cos – I got such a vivid picture in my head. Family portrait – two strapping girls –

LORNA. Yes!

ALLAN. I mean – I get it now! That *need*, you said.

LORNA. You understand.

ALLAN. And there I was, walking back, thinking we could give it a go.

LORNA (*delighted*). You mean it?

ALLAN. That's what I thought, out there –

LORNA. We can – you're right! (*Runs to hug him.*)

ALLAN. Not so much though, now.

He finds a cardboard box, emptied from LORNA*'s packing, and starts to pack* LORNA*'s dolls.*

LORNA. What are you / doing?

ALLAN. If you have to go, let's get this over with. I hate goodbyes.

LORNA. Go?

ALLAN. I'll drive you somewhere in the van.

LORNA. I don't want to go.

ALLAN. Oh, I don't want you to either. I love you more than anyone – hundreds and thousands of times more, but –

LORNA. I love you too.

ALLAN. – but we just can't have a future without trust, can we?

LORNA. Allan, please –

ALLAN. And if what Tiggy says is / true –

LORNA. Stop packing.

ALLAN. – then that's not good, sweetheart.

LORNA. I know, I know, / but

ALLAN. There's things where I need you on / my side –

LORNA. Please, listen to / me –

ALLAN. And if you can't do that then I don't think / we can –

LORNA. She stole it, Allan! She – she stole the coat from me.

A beat.

TIGGY. What?

ALLAN. Stole it, did she? Sounds like her.

TIGGY. I never stole / anything –

ALLAN. And those chains are unlocked.

LORNA. She forced me.

TIGGY. No. Stop it!

LORNA. She said she'd – hurt me.

TIGGY. Stop it, please.

LORNA. Kick me, scratch / me.

TIGGY. No, she's / lying!

LORNA. Punch me, cut me up and / then –

ALLAN holds up a hand for them to be quiet, and they are.

ALLAN. Good.

Thank you, Lorna, for explaining things.

Picking up TIGGY*'s chains, he goes to put them back on.*

TIGGY (*to* LORNA). But she knows – she knows I never / took anything –

Silently, ALLAN *takes the flowers and coat from* TIGGY. *He puts her ankle chains back on.*

ALLAN. If I could borrow your keys.

LORNA *fumbles for her keys and hands them over.* ALLAN *unlocks the cellar door.*

LORNA. What –

What are you going to do, love?

ALLAN. I'm going to take her downstairs.

Then – have some cocoa, d'you think? Listen to the wireless. Update my scrapbook.

LORNA. Your scrapbook? That sounds nice, can I / help – ?

ALLAN. No. Classified information.

Come on, witch –

He guides TIGGY *downstairs and is about to go down after her.*

LORNA. Allan. I'm – sorry –

ALLAN. Whatever for?

LORNA (*approaching him*). Whatever you want. Let's just have tea and cuddles.

ALLAN (*backing away*). It was a simple question, Lorn. And now it's answered.

Let's leave it at that.

He remembers he is still holding LORNA*'s keys in his hand.*

She sees them too and puts her hand out to receive them back.

He shakes his head. Puts them in his own pocket.

He goes into the cellar and shuts the door gently behind him. Then locks it.

EIGHT

A fortnight later. A dark and muggy morning.

ALLAN *is in the front room, playing Battleships on his own.*

He moves from one side of the table to the other, being both player and opponent.

LORNA *enters in her dressing gown. She sits down opposite* ALLAN, *offering to play with him.*

As she stretches out a hand to move a piece, he pulls the board away from her.

She tries again. He packs up the game and carries it out of the room.

A beat, then she follows him out like a hungry dog.

NINE

A fortnight later. Daytime, at summer's lowest ebb. Rain.

A bitter silence in the house.

ALLAN *is sitting at the table, eating a steak dinner.* LORNA *is opposite, gazing at him.*

She's still just wearing her dressing gown, now dirty. She has sleeplessness etched on her face.

TIGGY *is sitting in her 'naughty spot', head down.*

ALLAN *reaches for the salt. It's just out of arm's length and he can't get it.*

LORNA *rushes to fetch it for him. Salts his food for him, then sits, watching him.*

LORNA. I *love* you, Allan.

More today than yesterday. More than the day / before –

ALLAN. Yep, heard it. And what d'you expect me to do about it?

LORNA. Say it back, perhaps?

ALLAN (*grumpy*). Hm.

LORNA. Or, you know, you could –

(*Coyly.*) The business.

ALLAN. Oh, the business – it's buggered, if things go on like this.

Endless rain. No one's buying. Got a backlog of Fab lollies I can't shift for the life of me.

(*Pushes his plate away.*) Washing up, Tiggy.

Bring me afters. And don't you dare think of helping yourself.

TIGGY *goes to pick up the plate.*

(*Remembering the steak knife.*) Oh – and I'll take that, thank you –

He takes the knife off the plate. TIGGY *carries the plate out.*

ALLAN *goes to sit on the sofa.* LORNA *finds a footstool and places it gently beneath his feet, as he did for her in Scene One. She tries to touch him again and he edges away. She is close to tears.*

LORNA. A month –

A month, love. I can't sleep in that bed on my own.

Is it – her? It can't be her, not *still* –

I told you, I hate her.

ALLAN. Please. You don't know what hate is.

LORNA. So explain it to me.

ALLAN (*getting up*). I'm going to play trains.

LORNA. No, stay –

ALLAN. Tell Tiggy to bring the afters upstairs.

LORNA. – show me your – your scrapbook, or something?

ALLAN. See you / later.

LORNA. No, but I dare you! I dare you to show me – now you've got to.

Please, Allan, talk to me.

A beat. ALLAN *considers.*

Then goes to a high shelf and takes down a scrapbook. It is tightly bound with the same farmyard twine used to tie TIGGY*'s hands in Scene One.*

He unties it and unbinds it, and throws the book in front of LORNA, *sulkily.*

ALLAN. There, if you must. Starts at 1980, when we got –

LORNA (*looking at a photograph*). Oh – the van!

ALLAN. Bedford CA Morrison Electrofreeze.

LORNA (*overenthusiastic*). How lovely! And that's you in the window, with your mum?

ALLAN (*proud*). Look at her. Now *that's* nice hair, isn't it? It was long. Smooth. Felt like satin when she let me stroke it.

See, it was all still good then, before – (*Turns the page.*)

Piece of scarf, what we found Tiggy wound up in.

Note from Dad, the day he ran off, cos he couldn't bear the brat's wailing any more.

Then, we start – (*Turns page after page.*) souvenirs, see? Of a million little injuries.

LORNA. Souvenirs?

ALLAN. Rusty nail Tiggy put in my shoe.

When I tried to get her back for that she told on me, and Mum threw me out the house. Poor Mum's mind was poisoned.

(*Turns a page.*) That's the broken glass she hid in my mittens.

(*Turns a page.*) Bit of grain sack I slept on for a week – the summer I was fourteen.

LORNA. Why – ?

ALLAN. Tiggy fibbed that I was stealing ice creams from Dad's old freezer. Got me chucked out for ages that time – I slept in the yard for six nights.

By the time I broke in again there was a new lock on Mum's bedroom door, and she was inside, crying – she cried a lot, then. Said no one should come in, ever again.

One night, I – (*Turns the page, sees a drawing.*) ah, yes. Here.

I woke up, sick on myself. And I wanted, so much, for Mum to make it better.

I went and knocked on her door.

But that little witch had wormed her way in there, and she wouldn't open up, so, I – (*Points to a picture.*) I drew it all in my best felt tips, what I caught through the keyhole.

Record player, crackling, see? Smell of radiator dust, and pot pourri, and talc.

Poor Mum at the dressing table, in a daze. Tiggy, stood behind, with scissors.

Chattering her silly stories.

And strips of long hair, falling on the floor. Mum's lovely –

(*Points to the book.*) I drew it all, in case I ever ran out of the rocket fuel.

LORNA. The – the what?

ALLAN (*closes the book and binds it up again, puts it away*). Oh, the rocket fuel.

The real hate. See, it's not thin and bitter like yours, it's –

So sweet. Fizzes in you like sherbet, to keep you burning.

A beat, then:

I miss my mum.

LORNA. I know you do.

She goes to touch him. He backs away.

ALLAN. No, no, I'm alright. I'm still here, aren't I?

The witch didn't win out, in the end. I did.

Say I've won, Lorna.

LORNA. Oh, you've won, love.

And I'd say you've been very lenient with her, then, all things told. If I were you, I'd've –

ALLAN. What?

What would you do, then?

LORNA. Well, given her a jolly good smack, I suppose. Right across the knuckles.

ALLAN. A smack? Is that all?

LORNA. Oh –

God, no, of course not *all*. I mean –

How about a Chinese burn? – Remember from school?

ALLAN (*laughs*). A Chinese burn! I like that, sweetheart.

LORNA (*pleased*). You do?

ALLAN. What else?

He sits down on the sofa. Taps his lap, for her to come to him. She does, delighted.

LORNA (*trying to kiss him*). I knew you'd come / round –

ALLAN (*pushing her face away*). I said what else then?

LORNA. Oh, I don't know. Box her ears.

Wash her mouth out with soap –

ALLAN (*unimpressed*). Soap?

(*Pushes her away, gets up.*) I'm going upstairs – (*Heads out.*)

LORNA. No, no wait! I can do better –

ALLAN. See you / later –

LORNA. Yank – yank a clump of hair, out at the roots. Whip! – like that. How about it?

She takes his hand and tries to lead him back to the sofa. He resists.

A thwack round the arse with a stick.

ALLAN. Nails in it?

LORNA. If that's what's needed.

ALLAN. Good. Yes.

LORNA. Or, ooh, I know! A snip with scissors – the skin between fingers.

ALLAN (*laughs*). Ouch! That's got to smart.

LORNA. Oh, it stings like a bitch, I know.

ALLAN. But she'd deserve it?

LORNA. Of course she would. The lying witch.

ALLAN. That's it. What else?

LORNA. A punch in the guts with keys in your knuckles. I've done that.

ALLAN (*laughing*). Really? I'm impressed.

LORNA. Yes! Head down the toilet, flushed. Or a plastic bag on her head till she's grasping for air.

Here, sit with me.

He lets her pull him onto the sofa. They start to cuddle.

Bleach in her tea? A – a boiling kettle on her bare face. Kiss me, Allan –

ALLAN (*pushes her face away*). More –

LORNA. Make her lap up paint. Put drawing pins in her dinner.

ALLAN. Yes! (*Kisses her, a peck on the cheek.*)

LORNA. Force wet fingers to the plug socket! Cigarette burns in the palm of her hand! Or just –

A broken glass, smashed and jabbed, and tearing a furrow through her flesh like a – like a plough. Salt in the wound, every day, imagine that –

He kisses her fully on the lips. When she pulls away he is grinning.

Ah! Look! – I missed that. Toothy grin.

They cuddle. Tender and gentle and soft.

ALLAN. Teeth. Now she wouldn't need all her teeth, would she?

LORNA (*laughs, touching his face gently*). Definitely not.

ALLAN. Nor *both* ears.

LORNA (*laughs*). Oh! – Or or or –

Next time she tells tales, Allan – lop off her vicious little tongue.

ALLAN *laughs. Then the smile fades. A beat –*

– broken by TIGGY*, entering with a Fab lolly for* ALLAN*, on a plastic party plate.*

TIGGY. I brought afters.

The doorbell rings. ALLAN *and* LORNA *jump up.*

ALLAN (*looking out the window*). Shit. Stay here.

LORNA. No, don't leave me with / her –

ALLAN. It's fine, she'll go downstairs. (*To* TIGGY.) What does Big Bell mean?

LORNA. Allan, let me come with / you –

ALLAN (*to* LORNA). I won't be long. Tiggy –

ALLAN *points* TIGGY *to the cellar door.* TIGGY *hesitates.*

He takes the steak knife from the table and jabs at her threateningly.

She backs away and heads for the cellar door.

ALLAN *tucks the knife in his back pocket, conceals it, and goes out, shutting the door behind him.*

LORNA *goes to follow him but he has locked it.*

She goes to the window to try and see who it is. TIGGY *tries to grab her –*

TIGGY. Did you see the knife?! He'll slice us up this time –
we've got to get out!

We can get away if we work together.

LORNA *laughs*.

Tell him what you think of him! Then he'll have to let us out
of / here –

LORNA. For God's sake, there's no such thing as 'us'. There
never was.

TIGGY. No. Change your mind. I dare you –

LORNA *turns her back on* TIGGY, *goes back to the*
window.

You're a coward, then. You're a selfish / coward.

LORNA. Hey, watch your mouth.

TIGGY. I won't! And you can't make me, you old troll.

I'll put a curse on you!

On you and all your ugly – (*Goes to* LORNA*'s dolls*.)

LORNA. Oi, don't you touch those –

TIGGY *takes a doll from the shelf and puts it on the ground*.

I said / don't –

TIGGY *stamps on its head*.

No!

LORNA *rushes to the doll and tries to recover the pieces*.

As she's distracted, TIGGY *goes to the door of the room and*
tries to get out. She bangs on it.

TIGGY. Hello?!

LORNA. What are you / doing?

TIGGY. Hello! Please!

LORNA. Tiggy – / no!

LORNA grabs her by the hair and pulls her back from the door, as ALLAN comes back in.

Seeing him, TIGGY pulls away from LORNA's grasp and runs away down the cellar steps.

ALLAN smiles. Shows LORNA a leaflet from the caller.

ALLAN. 'Can I rely on your vote?' I said you can rely on nothing except yourself –

LORNA (*scared, breathless*). Did you – Did you see that?

She was yelling! If he'd heard her, or if –

ALLAN. Shhh, calm down.

LORNA. – oh God, if that had been Jonathan!

Or if she escaped somehow.

ALLAN. She won't escape.

LORNA. Imagine though, Allan.

If she talks now, I'll lose you. I can't bear that again!

ALLAN. It's fine, she knows the rules.

LORNA. No, it's not enough –

She's got to be stopped, properly –

ALLAN. Shh, love –

LORNA. – or we'll be cursed. You have to do it.

ALLAN. Do what?

LORNA. Cut it out –

Cut it out of her. Her lying, hateful, cursing little –

She covers her mouth, shocked at herself.

Impulsively, though, she rings the little bell on the table. ALLAN is excited – a kid fighting temptation.

ALLAN. I – I can't do that. Can I?

LORNA. Yes. Quick before I –

ALLAN. I'd make a mess! Mum's best carpet.

LORNA. Necessary, though. Or she'll spew everything, sooner or later.

And if people don't know you like I do then they could misunderstand –

ALLAN. What's going on here, of course. But –

LORNA. They won't even let you put your side of the story. She'll say you're a menace.

Oh, you've put up with her lies. You've cared for her. But would she say that? No!

Just think of it – it'd be all 'you're a bully, a misogynist, you're mean' –

TIGGY *enters nervously. She stops dead, surprised by the danger in* LORNA*'s words, as she continues.*

– 'You're cruel. You're a stupid thug. You don't even deserve any justice –

You deserve to lose everything you've got. Including me. Including *me*.

Then you'll die alone. Allan, have you thought about that? No one to look after you.

Because – oh – 'you're good for nothing but hating and hurting and hitting and' –

TIGGY *is laughing. The nervous but gleeful giggle of a child being given permission to be naughty.*

TIGGY. She –

She did, didn't she?

ALLAN. Did what?

TIGGY. She – changed. She said –

ALLAN. What's anything she says got to do with you?

TIGGY. Because – (*Looks to* LORNA, *smiling.*) because it's true.

That you're stupid.

That's why no one likes you. Even my mum didn't like you.

ALLAN. She wasn't your mum, she was / mine.

TIGGY. No, no, mine only. Mine to take for my own.

Cos you didn't deserve her.

Never clever, never fun, and so fat and sickly she couldn't bear to see you at the end.

That's why she told me, 'Lock the door'. Lock the door!'

ALLAN. Stop talking / now.

TIGGY (*a torrent, unstoppable*). Because she didn't want you near her, *touching* her – she told me to cut off her hair cos she couldn't bear you pawing at her and clawing and leeching, she said. And she forgot she even had you at the end, you know that?

She didn't care who you were or where you were she just thanked the gods that they'd sent me to her instead, cos she loved me hundreds and thousands of times / more –

ALLAN (*taking the steak knife out again*). You're sure about that, are you?

TIGGY. Yes! Didn't you know it? Dumbo!

TIGGY *laughs, looks to* LORNA, *encouraging her to laugh too.*

And you know what? You *will* die on your own – sad and screaming like a drowning wolf with a belly full of rocks cos –

She'll go too. Both of us will.

Just as soon as I've had my afters.

She smiles at LORNA. *Opens the lolly, and extends her other arm to* LORNA. *An outstretched hand, a show of solidarity. But* LORNA *doesn't take it.*

ALLAN (*calmly*). It's time.

TIGGY. For what?

ALLAN. You won't talk like that again.

A beat. TIGGY *realises. She runs for the front door.*

ALLAN *chases her out.*

(*Offstage.*) You little goblin! I'll teach / you!

TIGGY (*offstage*). No! No! Please – I'm sorry – I promise – I promise you –

Out in the corridor, the sounds of a struggle.

Alone in the sitting room, LORNA *picks up the discarded lolly and eats it.*

She winces a little at the sounds outside, but stays seated until –

LORNA (*an idea*). Oh! – Wait. Wait there!

She goes back to her box of stuff, tucked away. Finds the pickling jar that contained her mum's eye.

Allan, I found this. I kept this.

(*Takes it out and hands it to* ALLAN, *beyond the doorway.*) Is it useful?

TEN

A few days later. A bright morning, after rain. Birdsong.

The curtains are open. LORNA *is standing by the window.*

She is dressed properly now – clean, neat clothes, covered by a pretty apron.

Underneath this, there is a big pregnancy-shaped bump. She lays one hand on it, protectively.

In the other she is holding the jar, in which TIGGY*'s tongue – pale and bloody – is now preserved.*

She swills the liquid around the jar and holds it up to the light, fascinated.

ALLAN *enters, carrying a toolbox and a short plank of wood.*

He goes to her. Kisses her. And, gently, removes the bump – a cushion – from her under her gown.

ALLAN. Patience.

　　He throws it back on the sofa, then goes out, and returns with a stepladder.

　　He opens it, climbs, and places the wood on two brackets already put on the wall – it's a short, high shelf. He secures the shelf on the brackets.

LORNA. Is she asleep?

ALLAN. Dopey. I've chained her to one of the pipes. She'll be fine. (*Finishes the shelf.*)

LORNA (*puts the jar on the shelf*). There.

ALLAN. Lolly, are you sure about this? People might see.

LORNA. Oh, we'll think of something to say.

And it's important that she knows it's there. If she can see she's got something to earn back she might be a little better behaved from now on.

The doorbell rings. LORNA *and* ALLAN *go to the window and look out.*

ALLAN (*tuts*). I'll get rid of him.

LORNA. No, I told him to come and try his suit on. And if she's definitely dozing – ?

LORNA *finds the baby monitor, turns it on. They listen. No sound.*

She nods to ALLAN, *as the doorbell rings again.* ALLAN *goes out to answer it.*

LORNA *turns the baby monitor off again and shoves it under a cushion as* JONATHAN *comes in.*

(*To* ALLAN). And, sweetheart – if you could fetch Jonathan's costume for the wedding –

ALLAN *nods, goes out again.* JONATHAN *is standing near the cellar door.*

JONATHAN. How are things? You said he was –

LORNA. Oh, fine. It's all fine now.

JONATHAN. You look better.

LORNA. You look tired.

JONATHAN. Do I? No, no, I'm great. I'm brilliant, actually.

Guess what. (*Proudly.*) Got that bloke off my back. Paid him off.

And I put down six months' rent on the shop in advance. What d'you think of that?

LORNA. Kate must be pleased.

JONATHAN. She's – yes, she'll come round.

LORNA. What d'you / mean – ?

JONATHAN. Never mind, never mind. I should thank you, Lorna. That little pot –

LORNA. How much did you get?

JONATHAN. Ah! – I thought you didn't like me to be vulgar.

Let's just say – (*Excited.*) I cleaned up! God, I'm good. I fucking / cleaned –

ALLAN *returns, carrying a suit on a hanger.* JONATHAN *notices this and checks his excitement.*

LORNA. 'Cleaned / up' – ?

JONATHAN. Yeah, I – erm – I cleaned it up, and I passed it on to a collector I knew.

LORNA. But – it was Allan's. Don't you think you should give him a cut?

ALLAN. A cut of what?

JONATHAN. Nothing.

LORNA. The ivory thing.

ALLAN. Ah, yes.

You know what? – I've got some furs in the loft you might like, now.

LORNA *laughs.*

JONATHAN. Yes, very funny, thank you.

ALLAN. One of those ashtrays made from a gorilla's hand. That's rare, fetch a good price –

In the cellar below, TIGGY *starts to bang on a pipe. It is an appeal to be let out.*

The sound starts quietly, weakly, as ALLAN *and* LORNA *give a brief nervous glance to each other.*

*JONATHAN is still near the cellar door, blocking their way
to it.*

JONATHAN. Really, I don't know why everyone seems to
think it was about the money.

I mean, it *was* about the money, but it was important –

ALLAN. Erm – right –

JONATHAN. They were threatening to smash up my shop. And
she'd have left me, you said so yourself –

*LORNA gives him the suit and tries to usher him away from
the door.*

LORNA. Here, try it on at / home –

JONATHAN (*resisting*). And apart from anything else the – the
potential damage to it here. *Flowers* kept in it, for God's
sake. Water! I had to take it, to rescue it from – (*Breaking off
as the noise gets louder.*) God, what *is* that?

A pause in the noise, in response to his raised voice.

ALLAN. What's what?

JONATHAN. That noise. Irritating.

ALLAN. Rats. Maybe.

JONATHAN. What, with – weapons? I don't think it's rats.

LORNA. No. Plumbing, isn't it?

JONATHAN. I'd've said –

ALLAN. Course it's plumbing. Ancient pipes.

I'll go and sort it out.

LORNA. No, wait –

ALLAN. Won't be a / sec –

LORNA. Wait – I want to do it. I want to go and sort it out this
time.

A beat.

ALLAN. I don't think you'd manage it, sweetheart.

LORNA. I do. I've picked up enough know-how from you.

ALLAN. It's not a matter of 'know-how' –

LORNA. And I've been thinking about it for ages, wanting to try.

Is that weird? Please let me.

ALLAN. Lolly, you haven't got anything to prove. And it's dirty work, sweetheart.

JONATHAN. Blimey, Allan – this is the twenty-first century. Girls do plumbing.

LORNA. Exactly. (*Goes to* ALLAN*'s toolkit and selects some tools.*)

I can and I will.

(*As the banging starts again.*) Keys please, love.

ALLAN *hands over the keys he confiscated in Scene Seven.*

LORNA *takes a pair of pliers, a saw and a screwdriver.*

She unlocks the door to the cellar and goes down the steps. The banging gets louder.

JONATHAN *hovers awkwardly as* ALLAN *tries to listen at the cellar door.*

JONATHAN. I'm sorry, I didn't mean to be rude –

It's just that you can't try and stop her. She's always been strong-minded.

ALLAN (*trying to listen*). Shush –

JONATHAN. Even when we were / kids –

ALLAN. Oh, what did you know? If you went off to your poncey school –

JONATHAN. Actually, it wasn't my choice to board. My granddad insisted he pay / so –

ALLAN. So you left her behind.

JONATHAN. We wrote all the time.

ALLAN. With your bloody / Dad –

JONATHAN. Look, if you don't know the circumstances you can't really judge –

The banging stops. JONATHAN *calms.* ALLAN *steps away from the cellar.*

Ah. Thank God.

A bit of peace.

ALLAN *gives* JONATHAN *the suit. Opens the lounge door for him to go.*

Allan, listen, I do hope we can put it behind us – that silly stuff before, I'm –

ALLAN. –

JONATHAN. Oh, I'm thinking of starting a book club. Maybe you could come along to that.

I know it's not very macho, generally, but I was imagining it'd be just books about – I don't know – wrestling or something. What d'you reckon?

ALLAN. Not much of a reader.

JONATHAN. I could come round to watch a match, then.

ALLAN. Haven't got a telly.

And there's no use smarming up to me, alright? I'm not giving you more of my stuff.

JONATHAN (*laughs*). No, you don't understand, that's not –

LORNA *has re-entered, wiping her hands on her apron. She locks the cellar door behind her.*

LORNA. So you want more bargains, do you?

JONATHAN. Ah, Lorn. You sorted it.

LORNA. What else do you need to rescue?

JONATHAN. I really didn't intend –

LORNA. If you're after junk you can have this – (*Finds a box, tucked away.*) Dad's medals in there, that you wanted.

JONATHAN. Thank you.

LORNA (*putting more stuff in the box*). His decanter, and the one cut glass that he didn't get to smash. Ah, and – (*Sees the tongue in the jar. Takes it down.*) Why don't you have this as well?

JONATHAN. What is it?

ALLAN. No, Lorna –

LORNA. A curiosity. For your curiosity shop. (*Tucking it in the box, out of sight.*)

JONATHAN. Good God, what is that?

LORNA. Allan's family were in medicine.

ALLAN. Put it back.

JONATHAN. Blimey. Grisly.

LORNA. A conversation piece.

JONATHAN. Actually, you're right. A dealer friend of mine had a monkey brain in his window last year. Hallowe'en display – bit naff – but it pulled in no end of trade.

ALLAN. I thought we wanted to keep it.

LORNA. But now I'm of a mind to be rid of it, love.

And Jonathan's family – share and share alike. For a small price, of course.

JONATHAN (*realising*). Oh – of course, yes – (*Fumbles for some cash from his wallet.*)

ALLAN. We don't need money. I can / provide.

LORNA (*taking the money*). That's plenty generous, thank you. May it be your good-luck charm for a better year.

Smiling, relaxed now, LORNA *unzips the cover over* JONATHAN'*s suit.* JONATHAN *begins to try on his outfit for the wedding.*

ELEVEN

About a week later. The night before the wedding.

ALLAN *enters the living room, carrying a tube of superglue.*

He finds LORNA'*s doll with the broken face. He finds the broken pieces on the floor.*

He sits down at the table and glues it lovingly back together.

From his pocket he takes a gift bow. He sticks it on the doll's head, as if it's a present.

He gently places the doll back on the shelf, somewhere where LORNA *will see.*

He tiptoes out.

TWELVE

Morning. The next day.

LORNA *is in her wedding dress, tipsy – a bottle of champagne and glasses on the table.*

JONATHAN *is wearing a three-piece suit.*

She is holding a hairbrush and hairpins out to him.

LORNA. Allan likes it smooth.

JONATHAN. We've only got ten minutes. She's just gone to pick up the kids and then she'll be back –

LORNA. So shut up and get on with it.

He takes the brush and starts to style her hair.

JONATHAN. I just don't want to annoy her. Things are still a bit – you know.

Today'll help, though – I don't think I've looked this smart since our graduation.

LORNA. That's pulling! Stop pulling.

JONATHAN. Sorry.

LORNA *reaches for some painkillers and drinks them down with her champagne.*

What's the matter? You seem nervous.

LORNA. Not me. Don't do nervous.

I just don't want to trip up, that's all.

You've got to promise to hold on to me, when we're going into church.

I don't really know how to do it, that – that *walking* thing brides do.

JONATHAN (*laughs*). Course you do.

LORNA (*spots the doll that* ALLAN *mended*). Oh – look –

Gets up and goes to it.

JONATHAN. It's just one foot in front of another. Same as everyone does, all the time.

All you've got to concentrate on is what's at the end of that aisle. Think of the future.

LORNA. Yes. Of course. (*Kisses the doll and puts it back on the shelf.*).

How am I looking, then?

He gives her a mirror. She checks her hair.

He has created something hideous – a side ponytail, perhaps. They laugh.

Ah, very classy! I've not seen anything that lopsided since Mum used to do it.

JONATHAN. Come on, I think it's a bit special.

ALLAN (*calling from upstairs*). Lorna? Can you come here a minute?

LORNA (*calling to him*). I'm in my frock!

ALLAN (*upstairs*). Oh, sod that. I can't tie my fucking dickie bow.

LORNA (*calling*). Jonathan can come.

ALLAN (*upstairs*). No, I don't want him – touching me.

LORNA (*to* ALLAN, *laughing*). Hang about.

(*To* JONATHAN.) Get your tie on. And clean those bloody shoes.

She puts a coat on over her wedding dress and goes upstairs.

JONATHAN *puts his tie on, then sits down on the sofa to shine his shoes. After a moment he realises he's sitting on something – under one of the cushions. He looks.*

The baby monitor.

He picks it up, remembers it with affection.

He turns it on. Silence. Then turns it off again. Puts it to one side.

A beat, then he considers –

Did he just hear something? He turns it on again.

From the monitor comes the sounds of TIGGY, *tied up in the cellar. Soft murmurs.*

He stares at it, confused. Shakes it. Turns it off. On again. And the sounds still come.

JONATHAN. That's – (*Laughs.*)

(*Calling.*) Lorna? Lorn!

LORNA (*upstairs*). What?

JONATHAN. How – how are you doing / this?

LORNA (*upstairs*). I can't come now, Jonathan. Just make some tea or something.

He examines the monitor, turns it over.

Then wanders round the room, trying to work out where the sound is coming from.

JONATHAN. Hello? (*Laughing.*) – Hello? Is someone –

TIGGY *starts murmuring louder. She is waking from a drugged sleep.*

What the – ?

Half-laughing and half-scared, JONATHAN *traces the noises to the cellar door.*

He puts an ear to the door. Realises.

He puts the monitor down and tries to open the door. It's locked. He rattles it. He starts to panic.

Shit. Hang on. Hang on!

He sees ALLAN*'s toolkit, still out. He finds a crowbar and gets the door open.*

He goes into the cellar. Through the baby monitor, we hear him downstairs.

(*Offstage.*) Jesus Christ! Jesus fucking –

Hang on, alright? Just –

Shhh – keep still – keep still – shhhh –

The sound of him trying to untie TIGGY. *After a moment,* LORNA *returns.*

LORNA (*approaching*). Sorry about that – getting a bit frisky.

I think it's the wedding dress. Anything that says 'virgin' is like red rag to a bull.

I suppose that's what ten years of Sunday school does to you.

Jonathan?

She puts her head round the door and sees he's not in the room. Goes out again.

Are you making tea?

I'll have mine Irish, I think. You're right, I am a bit nervous, after all.

JONATHAN *emerges from the cellar. He is supporting* TIGGY, *who stumbles and staggers.*

LORNA *comes in.* JONATHAN *gestures at her to be quiet.*

JONATHAN. Lorna! Thank God. Shut the door – shut the door! – Quick!

Slowly, LORNA *shuts the lounge door.* JONATHAN *is breathless – shocked – spluttering –*

I just – I've found –

Shit, I always said there was something weird about him! – I told you, Lorna!

LORNA. Oh, God –

JONATHAN. The cellar – some woman – gagged and drugged and –

Hiding her under your bloody nose!

LORNA. Jonathan –

JONATHAN. Fucking hell, *look* at her. We've got to get her out of here.

(*Looking round for his keys*.) Where's my fucking car keys, Lorna?!

LORNA. She can't leave here.

JONATHAN. What, d'you think it's better to call the police?

LORNA. No –

JONATHAN (*searching his pockets*). Shit – my mobile's in the van. You'll have to distract him while I go out.

LORNA. The front door's locked.

JONATHAN. So unlock it then.

LORNA. No, she can't leave here.

JONATHAN. Course she can.

LORNA. She can't leave. She's ours.

Beat. JONATHAN *stops, laughs*.

JONATHAN. Yours?

LORNA. We keep her, yes.

JONATHAN. I – I don't understand, you – ?

LORNA. I thought you were snoozing, Tiggy.

JONATHAN. What d'you mean, you 'keep her'?

LORNA. Oh, he doesn't sleep with her. God no. She's like his sister.

JONATHAN. You –

You *knew* about this?

LORNA. You've never seen her cos we have to hide her. Cos she can't be trusted.

TIGGY *shakes her head.*

I had to sedate her today. Even let her keep her chains off –

JONATHAN. But –

LORNA (*to* TIGGY). – and this is how you thank me?

JONATHAN. But how long – ?

LORNA. Oh, she's been here years.

And in need of someone like me, all that time.

I'm sorry you had to see her now, the state she's in, but it's all her own fault.

She's a sort of retard.

TIGGY *shakes her head.*

JONATHAN. You can't – you can't do this to her just cos she's – got learning difficulties –

LORNA. We had to discipline her. She tried to curse us.

JONATHAN. Jesus Christ. You've –

Have you totally lost it? I knew I should never have let you stay here –

LORNA. I'm fine, I'm good at it, look –

Back downstairs now, Tiggy. (*Kicks her.*)

JONATHAN. What the hell are you doing?

LORNA. I said go back to your / napping – (*Shoves her.*)

JONATHAN (*trying to restrain her*). Lorna, stop / it.

LORNA (*to* TIGGY). You're not going to get what you want, you know.

JONATHAN. What does she want?

TIGGY *goes to the shelf and picks up a jar like the one that held her tongue.*

She waves it at JONATHAN, *imploringly. Tries to speak.*

LORNA *laughs as she goes to the lounge door and locks it –*
a precaution.

LORNA. It's sort of funny, isn't it? She sounds like a bad
ventriloquist!

JONATHAN. No, it isn't funny. What's she trying to say?

LORNA. I suppose she wants you to help her get out of here.

JONATHAN. Of course I will.

LORNA. That's not all though.

JONATHAN (*to* TIGGY). Here, have my jacket.

LORNA. That's not all, I said.

JONATHAN. What's not all?

LORNA. I think these histrionics are supposed to mean –

JONATHAN. Where's my bloody car / keys?

LORNA. – that she wants her tongue back.

JONATHAN. Her what?

LORNA. Allan cut it out.

JONATHAN. Fucking hell –

LORNA. She wants you to bring it back.

JONATHAN. Me?

LORNA. You took it.

JONATHAN. I didn't take anyone's tongue, don't be insane. (*To*
TIGGY.) Let's go.

LORNA. She knows you / did.

JONATHAN. Lorna, stop / it –

LORNA. In the box.

JONATHAN. Shut up.

LORNA. In the jar.

A beat.

JONATHAN. Oh my God.

A beat.

TIGGY *tries to pull* JONATHAN *away but he takes a step back from her in shock.*

Oh God, no –

LORNA (*laughs*). What's the matter?

JONATHAN. Lorna –

LORNA. Hmm?

JONATHAN. You just let me take –

You never –

You didn't –

LORNA. Spit it out.

JONATHAN. You didn't – tell me! (*To* TIGGY.) She didn't tell me anything –

LORNA. It wasn't your business to know.

JONATHAN. Wasn't my business – ?

You made it my business! I've had that thing in my shop window –

A whole fortnight! *Shit.* People – gawping –

LORNA. Oh. Lovely.

JONATHAN. Taking pictures. Pointing –

LORNA. You hear that, Tiggy? –

JONATHAN. They'll think –

LORNA (*to* TIGGY). – you're famous.

JONATHAN. They'll think I'm part of this. They'll say I did this to her!

LORNA. Oh, don't be daft.

JONATHAN. Course they will! You're my sister. I've been round here all the time. Weeks and weeks! And then I go and –

LORNA. What?

JONATHAN. I sold it, Lorna. I fucking sold it.

LORNA (*laughs*). Oh dear.

JONATHAN. Shit –

LORNA. Who to?

JONATHAN. Some bloke. Asking questions. Asking about – paperwork –

LORNA (*directed at* TIGGY). So it's gone, then.

JONATHAN (*a new thought*). Oh God, he –

LORNA (*to* TIGGY). Too late.

JONATHAN. – he suspected, didn't he? That's why he was asking –

LORNA (*to* TIGGY). Back downstairs then.

TIGGY *shakes her head, backs away.*

JONATHAN. He's on to me – someone's on to me already. They'll close me down – arrest me. (*A new thought.*) Kate! – She'll –

As LORNA *closes in on her,* TIGGY *tries to pull* JONATHAN *away. He breaks away from her and paces, in his own private panic.*

She'll leave me! She'll do it this time – oh shit –

TIGGY *looks for a way out on her own. She tries the door, it's locked.*

LORNA. Tiggy, downstairs, now.

TIGGY *shakes her head, avoids* LORNA*'s grasp.*

JONATHAN. She already thinks I'm mixed up with violent – dodgy –

TIGGY *sees* LORNA*'s champagne glass. She grabs it.*

LORNA (*to* TIGGY). What are you doing?

TIGGY *smashes it against the table – holds the broken piece out towards* LORNA.

JONATHAN. She'll take the kids.

LORNA (*to* TIGGY). Alright, calm / down –

LORNA *tries to grab the glass from* TIGGY, *but* TIGGY *jabs at her hands, cutting her.*

LORNA *draws her hands away in pain.*

Ow! Jonathan –

JONATHAN. I'll never see them again, Lorna. My boys.

LORNA. – just give me a hand here, will you?

From outside, a beep on a car horn.

They all freeze for a second.

JONATHAN *runs to the window.*

JONATHAN. It's her. It's –

ALLAN (*calling, offstage*). Lorna, you ready?

JONATHAN. She can't see. (*Draws the curtains.*) She can't come in – I won't let the kids / see –

ALLAN (*calling, offstage*). Can I come down?

JONATHAN. Shit – shit – shit – I just need to think, alright? I just –

TIGGY, *hearing* ALLAN, *shakes her head.*

LORNA (*calling, to* ALLAN). Yes, come / down.

TIGGY *grabs* LORNA *by the hair and slams her head against the wall.*

Tiggy! Stop it!

TIGGY *closes in on her, holding the sharpest edge to* LORNA*'s throat.*

Really, this is all a waste of time.

He's not going to help you. Are you, Jonathan?

JONATHAN. Hm?

LORNA. D'you want to take her out of here?

JONATHAN. Take her – ?

LORNA. Oh, I mean, fine, if you want.

Leave with her, see if I care. Walk out and introduce her to your family.

JONATHAN. For God's sake –

LORNA. Do you want to help her or not?

JONATHAN. I can't –

LORNA. Cos you said that you / would.

JONATHAN. I don't care, I don't care, Lorna! I'm not going to have my whole life ruined by some fucking mental woman –

A beat. The sound of ALLAN *trying, then unlocking, the lounge door.*

Look, I didn't mean that. I'm sorry, I –

ALLAN (*outside the door*). Right, so where's this frock I've been waiting / to –?

He enters – sees TIGGY *with* LORNA.

What's going on? – (*Sees* JONATHAN.) Oh, I get what you're after.

This isn't the way though, Tigs. Leave off her.

TIGGY *shakes her head, tightens her grip.*

LORNA. Leave off me, he said.

Or we'll – (*A new idea, she smiles.*)

Oh, you know what? We'll have to let those old man-hunting monsters in here.

TIGGY *shakes her head.*

Yeah, you think they're not real, don't you? – But I lied.

TIGGY *shakes her head.*

'Fraid so. They're everywhere.

They chased me all the way here, when I came.

JONATHAN. What are you talking about / now?

LORNA. Grabbed me by my ankles. Flayed off my flesh – look!

She shows her the scar from where her dad cut her.

They gnawed at my neck, tried to saw off my head and suck my guts up through my throat like a straw.

JONATHAN. God, this is too fucking / weird –

LORNA. Shut / up.

JONATHAN. I need some air – can you unlock the front door –

LORNA. You'll be let out when I say so. Sit down.

Tell her, Allan. The cannibals are out there.

ALLAN. The cannibals are out there.

Uncertainty flickers across TIGGY*'s face, but she still shakes her head.*

LORNA. There you go. You see? – You shouldn't have trusted me.

They've just been hiding, the last few months, but –

(*Looks out of the window.*) Oh yes, they're closing in on the house, right now.

Heard all this fuss you've been making, and they've come to collect your head. Smuggle it away, like Mum said, under their tall hats.

And I can't protect you, Tiggy, if you don't let me go. Now can I?

TIGGY – *confused and afraid* – *loosens her grip on* LORNA, *but keeps the glass pointed at her.*

That's a good girl. Now give me that.

TIGGY *shakes her head.*

No? Let's see then. I wonder what's in the hall.

Allan, what's out in the hall?

ALLAN. Sweetheart, his missus is parked on the / driveway –

LORNA. Discipline, Allan. What's in the fucking hallway?

ALLAN *brings in two top hats from the hall outside.*

Look at that.

Must have been dropped by someone passing. Finders keepers though, eh?

Give one to Jonathan.

ALLAN *does.*

There you go, young man. What do you say?

JONATHAN. I don't know what's happening / here –

LORNA. It's putting on a hat. Put the fucking hat on.

ALLAN *and* JONATHAN *put the hats on. They look too big, distorted, strange.*

TIGGY *cowers at the sight.*

See, you've got to believe us, Tigs.

It's a pity, but it's a *fierce* little world out there, and no one likes girls who tell tall tales. So don't you think you'd be better off, where you are?

You don't want it all to change, do you? Let's keep things nice and safe.

TIGGY *hesitates again.*

The doorbell rings. It is too loud, too long. She covers her ears.

JONATHAN. That's –

LORNA. I think we all know who it is. (*To* TIGGY.) Don't we?

See, I can conjure them – I'm an enchantress!

Slowly, TIGGY *puts the glass down on the floor.* LORNA *grabs it.*

LORNA *nods to* ALLAN *to bring* TIGGY*'s wrist and ankle chains from the sideboard.*

He does, and LORNA *puts them on* TIGGY. JONATHAN *watches, takes off his hat, puts it down –*

JONATHAN. Look – I want to say something. I'm not happy about this.

If you're just treating this person as an inferior cos she's got learning difficulties then that's – then you can't do that – by law.

LORNA. Jonathan, I'm not worried about you.

JONATHAN. Well, you should be. Cos I know about this now / and I'm –

LORNA. And I know about you. I know you.

See, you can have your wife, and your cute kids. And your twee shop and your neat house. Smug Sunday lunches and big fat fucking newspapers and family fun days, and everyone in their place.

That's all you really want, isn't it? That's all that any of you want.

Else you'd curse and shout and rage.

You'd do something. And are you going to?

JONATHAN. I am, actually. I just need to think – I just need –

He trails off. LORNA *points to the 'naughty spot'.* TIGGY *goes to it and crouches.*

LORNA (*to* ALLAN). She's waiting. Go on.

ALLAN *leads* JONATHAN *out.*

Special treat, Tiggy, for a special day – you can stay up here.

To listen out for the Hatters. How's about that?

And we'll be back soon. Then you and me will have some playtime, alright?

LORNA *goes out, closing the door.* TIGGY *sits in the darkness, lit by a shaft of new sunlight through the curtains. It glows, brighter than it should. Blinding.*

A pause, then –

JONATHAN *rushes in again, breathless,* LORNA*'s keys in his shaking hands. He and* TIGGY *lock eyes.*

He finds his top hat and picks it up, as there is an impatient beep on the car horn outside.

He takes a step closer to TIGGY*. She tries to speak. As she does, her mouth fills up with blood.*

More blood than there could be. More blood than her mouth can hold. It spills out, down her neck.

JONATHAN *reaches to her. An outstretched hand. Their fingers touch.*

He smiles a faint smile. He opens his mouth to speak –

Lights down.

The End.

A Nick Hern Book

Hundreds and Thousands first published in Great Britain as a paperback original in 2011 by Nick Hern Books, 14 Larden Road, London W3 7ST, in association with Buckle for Dust

Cover image by Radford Wallis
Cover designed by Ned Hoste, 2H

Typeset by Nick Hern Books, London
Printed in the UK by CLE Print Ltd, St Ives, Cambs, PE27 3LE

A CIP catalogue record for this book is available from the British Library

ISBN   978 1 84842 212 4